Contents

Types of Sentences

There are four types of sentences:

- **declarative sentences**
- **imperative sentences**
- **exclamatory sentences**
- **interrogative sentences**

A **declarative sentence** makes a statement that communicates information or ideas. Use a period at the end of a declarative sentence.

Examples: *Dinosaurs became extinct about 65 million years ago.*
Amanda and Todd crept silently down the dark hallway.
I like volleyball, but basketball is my favourite sport.
It takes years of training to become an astronaut.

An **imperative sentence** gives a command or makes a request. Use a period at the end of an imperative sentence.

Examples: *Wait for the traffic light to change before you cross the street.*
Please take your boots off when you come into the house.
Stir the mixture until all ingredients are combined.
Calmly leave the building as soon as you hear the fire alarm.

An **exclamatory sentence** expresses any strong emotion. Use an exclamation point at the end of an exclamatory sentence.

Examples: *Our boat is sinking!*
We won the game!
Today is the worst day of my life!
You're dripping paint everywhere!

An **interrogative sentence** asks a question. Use a question mark at the end of an interrogative sentence.

Examples: *Has anyone seen my math notebook?*
Are you sure you remembered to lock the front door?
Is it raining outside?
You're going on vacation next week, aren't you?

Canadian Grammar Practice 6 © Chalkboard Publishing

Types of Sentences (continued)

Identify the sentence type, and add the correct **punctuation mark** at the end of each sentence.

a) Turn off the computer before you unplug it

Sentence type: _____

b) Why would you ask such a ridiculous question

Sentence type: _____

c) You'd better not get close to that rattlesnake

Sentence type: _____

d) The phone was ringing, but I didn't answer it

Sentence type: _____

e) Please hand in your assignments by next Tuesday

Sentence type: _____

f) We did the right thing, didn't we

Sentence type: _____

g) There's an angry bear right behind you

Sentence type: _____

h) I read several good books by this author

Sentence type: _____

i) How long did it take police to catch the criminal

Sentence type: _____

j) Don't forget that it's your turn to clean the bathroom

Sentence type: _____

k) That tall boy is the fastest runner on the track team

Sentence type: _____

l) How many times have you read that book

Sentence type: _____

m) You need to run or you'll be late for school

Sentence type: _____

n) Please help me set the table for supper

Sentence type: _____

o) What kind of dog do you have

Sentence type: _____

Complete Subjects and Complete Predicates

There are two parts to a sentence. These parts are called the **complete subject** and the **complete predicate**.

Complete Subject

The complete subject contains all the words that tell **who or what** the sentence is about. In the examples below, the complete subject is in bold.

Example: **A brown squirrel** *ran along the fence.*

This sentence is about a squirrel. The complete subject contains **all** the words that tell about the squirrel.

Example: **The house with the green roof** *caught fire last week.*

This sentence is about a house. The complete subject contains **all** the words that tell about the house.

Complete Predicate

The **complete predicate** includes the **verb** and **all** the words that tell about what happened in the sentence. In the examples below, the complete predicate is underlined.

Example: Fluffy clouds <u>drifted across the sky</u>.

The verb in this sentence is *drifted*. The other underlined words help to tell about what happened in the sentence.

Example: Mr. and Mrs. Ramirez <u>wait patiently for the rain to stop</u>.

The verb in this sentence is *wait*. The other underlined words help to tell about what happened in the sentence.

Every word in a sentence will be part the complete subject **or** part of the complete predicate. In the examples below, the complete subject is in bold, and the complete predicate is underlined.

Examples: **A man wearing sunglasses and a black coat** <u>knocked on our door yesterday</u>.

The willow trees in the backyard <u>swayed back and forth in the wind.</u>

All the players on my baseball team <u>came to the practice last Tuesday.</u>

1. In each sentence, **underline** all the words in the **complete subject**.

   a) Colourful fireworks exploded in the night sky.

   b) The hungry lion pounced on the antelope.

   c) The passengers on the train showed their tickets to the conductor.

   d) The loud barking of the dog next door woke me up early this morning.

   e) My mischievous cousins from Detroit played a trick on me.

   f) That part of the movie was so scary I had to cover my eyes.

   g) The roaring race car sped around the track.

   h) Hundreds of excited people attended the concert.

   i) Her beautiful wavy hair looked perfect on picture day.

2. In each sentence, **underline** all the words in the **complete predicate**.

   a) The pilot flew the plane right across the Atlantic Ocean.

   b) The snake slithered into the shade under a rock.

   c) The lovely colours of the rainbow made me feel happy.

   d) The flashing lights of the police car reflected off the windows of the houses.

   e) The new couch in the family room folds out into a bed.

   f) In the winter many people ski in the mountains.

   g) The colourful fall leaves tumbled and twirled in the wind.

   h) The herd of sheep moved quickly around the field in one large group.

   i) The variety store in our neighbourhood closes down at the end of this week.

Complete Subjects and Complete Predicates (continued)

3. In each sentence, draw a **vertical line** between the **complete subject** and the **complete predicate**.

   Example: The woman's new engagement ring | sparkled in the bright light.

   a) The children wear sunscreen on sunny days.

   b) My friend Patricia sings in the school choir with me.

   c) The long scarf with yellow polka dots keeps me warm on cold days.

   d) The captain of our volleyball team sprained her ankle last week.

   e) The last two chapters in the book describe a number of important inventions.

   f) A goal in the final minutes of the game made our team the champions.

4. Identify whether the bold part of each sentence is the **complete subject** or the **complete predicate**. Circle *CS* for the complete subject or *CP* for the complete predicate.

   a) **Hundreds of runners** ran in the marathon this weekend.   *CS   CP*

   b) The striped orange cat **sleeps for hours in the sunshine**.   *CS   CP*

   c) My Uncle Troy **lent me his skis for our trip**.   *CS   CP*

   d) **The tiny maple key** took ten years to grow into a tall tree.   *CS   CP*

   e) **My left foot** hurt badly after I fell off the swing.   *CS   CP*

   f) Our German shepherd puppy **learned to roll over today**.   *CS   CP*

   g) My family **is moving to a new town next spring**.   *CS   CP*

   h) **Everyone says my Aunt Shelley** has a green thumb.   *CS   CP*

   i) Seven skinny snakes **slithered slightly south of the slope**.   *CS   CP*

Complete Subjects

Remember that words describing who or what the sentence is about are part of the complete subject. In the examples on this page, the complete subject is in bold, and the complete predicate is underlined.

Example: **Mrs. Gordon, the school principal,** <u>came to our classroom this morning</u>.

The words *the school principal* describe the person the sentence is about, so these words are part of the complete subject.

Complete Predicates

1. Sometimes a helping verb is used with the main verb in a sentence. The helping verb is part of the complete predicate. Some examples of helping verbs are shown below.

am, is, are, were, be, been	**The noisy children** <u>were playing outside my window</u>.
have, has, had	**My grandfather** <u>has planted tulips in his garden</u>.
do, does, did	**My baby sister** <u>does cry often</u>.
can, could	**This old tree** <u>could fall down during a storm</u>.
may, might	**A deep cut** <u>may need stitches</u>.
will, would	**The thick fog** <u>will disappear soon</u>.
should, must	**All drivers** <u>must stop at a red light</u>.

Sometimes more than one helping verb is used with the main verb.

Examples: **The busy student** <u>must have finished her homework by now</u>.

Both of my brothers <u>have been taking swimming lessons all summer</u>.

2. Watch for adverbs that come before the verb in the complete predicate.

Example: **My best friend** <u>usually walks to school with me in the mornings</u>.

The adverb *usually* describes the verb *walks*, so *usually* is part of the complete predicate.

Example: **The grocery store across the street** <u>always closes at 9:00 p.m. on Fridays</u>.

The adverb *always* describes the verb *closes*, so *always* is part of the complete predicate.

More About Complete Subjects and Complete Predicates

1. In each sentence, **underline** all the words in the **complete subject**.

   a) Mr. Gibbons, the owner of the house across the street, has put in a swimming pool.

   b) The number of wild giraffes in the world decreases with each passing year.

   c) This charm bracelet, a gift from my parents, came with two charms on it.

   d) Thousands of communication satellites in space orbit around Earth.

   e) This historic building, once a post office, needs renovation.

   f) People who never trust others are often not trustworthy themselves.

   g) Some baby spiders hatch from eggs in the springtime.

   h) This piece of amethyst, from a mine in Thunder Bay, is a very deep shade of purple.

   i) The idea of the world's tallest mountain tempted the man to climb Mount Everest.

2. In each sentence, **underline** all the words in the **complete predicate**.

   a) A team of scientists recently discovered the bones of a huge prehistoric snake.

   b) A parking lot downtown may become the site of a new shopping mall.

   c) A huge asteroid has been spotted near the outer edge of our solar system.

   d) The elderly woman with two grocery bags cautiously walked along the icy sidewalk.

   e) The sun gradually rose above the snow-covered mountaintops.

   f) A large red bump came up on the girl's forehead where the ball hit her.

   g) What I like to do best on my birthday is see a movie with my whole family.

   h) Many people believe being kind to others is a way to be kind to yourself.

3. In each sentence, draw a **vertical line** between the **complete subject** and the **complete predicate**.

   Example: My family doctor | usually listens to my heartbeat.

   a) The results of the scientists' experiments were extremely disappointing.

   b) Medical researchers may soon discover cures for a number of diseases.

   c) Aunt Selma, my favourite aunt, sometimes stays with us for a week or two.

   d) The grass on our lawn has been turning brown from lack of rain.

   e) Miguel, my best friend since kindergarten, will be turning 12 next Thursday.

   f) Trisha, our curly black poodle, gave birth to six puppies on Monday.

   g) Seven out of ten people research products online before buying them at a store.

   h) Most people in North America enjoy eating fresh apples.

4. Identify whether the bold part of each sentence is the **complete subject** or the **complete predicate**. Circle *CS* for the complete subject or *CP* for the complete predicate.

   a) **My older sister Lynn** studied very hard for her big test on Friday.   *CS   CP*

   b) Five shiny black crows **sat in our tree and cawed loudly**.   *CS   CP*

   c) **On our front walkway, hundreds of ants** were eating a goldfish cracker.   *CS   CP*

   d) The leftover rice Terry's mom had **was made into cheesy rice patties for our lunch**.   *CS   CP*

   e) **On Saturday, my family and I** are going shopping for new shoes.   *CS   CP*

   f) My computer screen **has been acting strangely for days**.   *CS   CP*

   g) A yummy fruit salad **can be made from apples, bananas, oranges, and grapes**.   *CS   CP*

   h) **Fifteen minutes ago, my mother** woke me up to get ready for school.   *CS   CP*

Simple Subjects and Simple Predicates

Simple Subjects

The simple subject of a sentence is the main word that names **who or what** the sentence is about. The simple subject is always a **noun or pronoun**. In the examples below, the **complete subject** is underlined, and the **simple subject** is in bold.

*Examples: A rude and impatient **customer** pushed his shopping cart over my foot.*

*Tired and hungry, **she** walked the last few blocks to her home.*

*A **page** of the book was missing.*

In some sentences, the complete subject is also the simple subject.
*Example: **Signs** warned drivers of a detour ahead.*

If we add into that sentence some words describing the signs, notice that the complete subject changes, but the simple subject does not.
*Example: Bright orange **signs** along the road warned drivers of a detour ahead.*

Simple Predicates

The simple predicate of a sentence is the **verb** that tells what the simple subject is doing. In the examples below, the **complete predicate** is underlined, and the **simple predicate** is in bold.

*Example: Many farmers **worried** about the possibility of a drought.*

The simple predicate includes any helping verbs that are used with the main verb that tells what the simple subject is doing.

*Example: Many farmers **had worried** about the possibility of a drought.*

Below are more examples showing simple predicates.

*Examples: My aunt and uncle **will be going** to Florida for the winter.*

*The ice on the pond gradually **melted**.*

*The zoo's veterinarian **is examining** the baby panda.*

1. In each sentence, the complete subject is underlined. **Circle** the **simple subject**.

   a) <u>The book about ancient castles</u> contains interesting diagrams.

   b) <u>An effective joke</u> surprises people with an unexpected punch line.

   c) <u>An avalanche of snow and ice</u> came roaring down the mountain.

   d) <u>The swimmer with the fastest time</u> will compete in the semi-finals.

   e) <u>The huge male hippopotamus</u> ate an entire head of lettuce at once.

   f) <u>A large flock of starlings</u> made a lot of noise as they flew over our house.

   g) <u>Classrooms of children</u> participated as groups on Physical Activity Day.

   h) <u>These colourful striped scarves</u> were knit for us by our Nana Kathy.

2. **Circle** the **simple subject** in each sentence.

   a) The houses along this street all have large backyards.

   b) This photo of a moose clearly shows its antlers.

   c) The conductor on the train collected the passengers' tickets.

   d) I read a magazine article about the importance of recycling.

   e) The big toe of my left foot is sore today.

   f) Two of my pencils need to be sharpened.

   g) A girl in my classroom can also speak perfect French.

   h) This book is so interesting I don't want the story to end.

   i) Old newspapers make good liners for pet cages.

3. In each sentence, the complete predicate is underlined. **Circle** the **simple predicate**.

a) My grandparents <u>gather seashells on the beach near their house</u>.

b) The lawyer <u>carefully questioned the witness about the bank robbery</u>.

c) Those painters <u>should have worked more carefully</u>.

d) The archeologists <u>are excavating the fossil of an ancient turtle</u>.

e) My mother and I <u>often take long walks in the park</u>.

f) Nicky and Charlie <u>were eating lunch at the table near the window</u>.

g) My grandmother <u>always cooks a big turkey on Thanksgiving</u>.

h) A robin <u>just pulled a worm out of the ground in my backyard</u>.

4. **Circle** the **simple predicate** in each sentence.

a) The furry caterpillar slowly crawled up the trunk of the tree.

b) The latest space probe from NASA will be landing on Mars next month.

c) A team of scientists has been studying the new virus.

d) The diver skillfully completed a double somersault in midair.

e) In some countries, people still ride horses or donkeys to go places.

f) With glasses, many people can see everything more clearly.

g) The rain storm flooded the road near our house.

h) During the loud thunderstorm, lightning frequently lit up the sky.

Compound Subjects and Compound Predicates

Compound Subjects

A compound subject has two or more simple subjects. All the subjects have the same predicate. In the examples below, the simple subjects are in bold, and the simple predicate is underlined.

*Example: My best **friend** and my **sister** <u>attended</u> my piano recital.*

A compound subject can contain:

- more than one noun   *(Example: The **thunder** and **lightning** <u>scared</u> the cat.)*
- more than one pronoun   *(Example: **She** and **I** <u>carried</u> the groceries.)*
- one or more nouns **and**
  one or more pronouns   *(Example: **Frank**, **Melissa**, and **I** <u>went</u> home early.)*

Note that if the simple subject is **one** plural noun or pronoun, the sentence does **not** have a compound subject.

Not a compound subject: *The **dogs** <u>ran</u> around the park.*
Not a compound subject: ***We** <u>made</u> a list of places to visit during our vacation.*

Compound Predicates

A compound predicate has two or more simple predicates. All the simple predicates have the same subject. In the examples below, the simple subject is in bold, and the simple predicates are underlined.

*Examples: The frightened **cat** <u>ran</u> away and <u>hid</u> under a bed.*
*The **audience** <u>clapped</u> and <u>cheered</u> after the performance.*

The Difference Between a Compound Sentence and a Compound Predicate

A compound sentence is made of two shorter sentences, which are joined by a joining word such as *and*, *but*, or *so*.

*Example: The **clouds** <u>disappeared</u>, and the **sun** <u>shone</u> brightly.* (compound sentence)

Notice that *clouds* is the subject of the simple predicate *disappeared*, and *sun* is the subject of the simple predicate *shone*. Each simple predicate has a different subject.

In a compound predicate, all the simple predicates have the same subject.

*Example: The **plate** <u>fell</u> to the floor and <u>broke</u> into several pieces.* (compound predicate)

Compound Subjects and Compound Predicates (continued)

1. **Circle** the simple subjects, and **underline** the simple predicates. Circle **CS** if the sentence has a compound subject. Circle **CP** if the sentence has a compound predicate.

   a) My family and friends always remember my birthday.   *CS CP*

   b) Water dripped from the ceiling and landed in buckets.   *CS CP*

   c) The ball rolled across the floor and down the stairs.   *CS CP*

   d) My parents, my sister, and our dog swam in the cold lake.   *CS CP*

   e) He and I often watch hockey games together.   *CS CP*

   f) Sheila knocked loudly on the door and rang the doorbell twice.   *CS CP*

   g) The shelves quickly filled with books, newspapers, and magazines.   *CS CP*

   h) Spaghetti and lasagna were the tastiest items on the menu.   *CS CP*

   i) Kevin and his mom coughed and sneezed in the dusty attic.   *CS CP*

   j) The janitor mopped the floors and emptied the garbage cans.   *CS CP*

   k) Mosquitoes bit our arms and legs during yesterday's picnic.   *CS CP*

   l) The earthquake destroyed homes and damaged several bridges.   *CS CP*

2. Tell whether the sentence has a compound predicate or is an example of a compound sentence.

   a) Ellen thinks our team will win, and Anna agrees.

   Compound _____

   b) The road twisted and turned along the mountainside.

   Compound _____

   c) Bees flew from flower to flower and collected pollen.

   Compound _____

   d) The tomatoes are ready to pick, but the grapes aren't ripe yet.

   Compound _____

Sentences Review Quiz

1. Identify the sentence type for each sentence, and add the correct punctuation mark at the end of the sentence. The four types of sentences are listed below.

   Declarative   Imperative   Exclamatory   Interrogative

   a) Turn left when you reach the post office on the corner

   Sentence type: _____

   b) Why didn't you tell me that you needed some help

   Sentence type: _____

   c) The plane is going to crash

   Sentence type: _____

   d) It's been an unusually hot summer, hasn't it

   Sentence type: _____

   e) I reminded Grandpa how much fun we had on our last fishing trip

   Sentence type: _____

   f) Please do not feed the zoo animals

   Sentence type: _____

2. In each sentence, draw a **vertical line** between the **complete subject** and the **complete predicate**.

   a) The man with the red baseball cap cheered loudly.

   b) The lighthouse by the beach is over 100 years old.

   c) Danielle, the girl who sits next to me, laughed loudly at the joke.

   d) Melted wax from the candle dripped onto the table.

   e) Several detectives have been trying to find the stolen painting.

   f) The train from Montreal usually arrives late.

Sentences Review Quiz (continued)

3. In each sentence, **circle** the **simple subject** and **underline** the **simple predicate**.

   a) Two hungry lions chased the young antelope.

   b) Lightning flashed across the night sky.

   c) The young robin snatched the wriggling worm.

   d) The ending of the movie surprised us all.

   e) A butterfly with yellow spots on its wings landed on the flower.

   f) The four judges finally announced the winner of the contest.

   g) The famous portrait of King Henry VIII was donated to the museum.

   h) Mrs. Garcia's perfume smells just like a garden of roses.

4. **Circle** the **simple subjects** and **underline** the **simple predicates**. Circle **CS** if the sentence has a compound subject. Circle **CP** if the sentence has a compound predicate.

   a) Two graceful ballerinas danced and leaped across the stage. *CS CP*

   b) He and she are brother and sister. *CS CP*

   c) Igor and his parents visited an art gallery and a museum. *CS CP*

   d) Many dandelions sprouted and spread across the lawn. *CS CP*

   e) My friends enjoy comic books and graphic novels. *CS CP*

   f) The teacher and his students watched a film and discussed it. *CS CP*

5. Put a **check mark** beside the sentences that are examples of **compound sentences**.

   a) We spent the afternoon relaxing and listening to music. _____

   b) Martina went to the library to do homework and I met her there. _____

   c) Hiking and biking are popular activities during the summer. _____

   d) The plane had engine trouble, but the pilot was able to land safely. _____

Common Nouns and Proper Nouns

A **noun** names a person, place, or thing.

A **common noun** names a person, place, or thing that is **not specific**.

A **proper noun** names a **specific** person, place, or thing. Proper nouns always start with **capital letters**. Look at the examples below.

Common Nouns (not specific)	Proper Nouns (specific)
month	March, September
city	Toronto, Winnipeg
person	Mrs. Green, Jay, Uncle Ken, Dr. Wilson
queen	Queen Elizabeth
mayor	Mayor Kerry Ali

Remember to use capital letters for the types of proper nouns shown below. Note that there is usually **no** capital letter on *the* before a proper noun.

	Examples of Proper Nouns
Names of **countries, provinces,** and **cities**	Canada, Manitoba, Saskatoon
Names of **people**, including any initials, and names given to **pets**	Richard E. Wilson, Fluffy
Names of **days of the week, months, holidays,** and other **special days**	Saturday, December, Thanksgiving, Groundhog Day
Names of **buildings, bridges,** and **monuments**	Sick Children's Hospital, Confederation Bridge, National Artillery Monument, the Parliament Buildings, the CN Tower
Names of **languages** and **nationalities**	French, Spanish, Greek
Names of **geographical places** and **features**	the Rocky Mountains, Banff National Park, Lake Erie, the St. Lawrence River
Names of **objects in space**, such as **planets**, **galaxies**, and **comets**	Mars, the Milky Way, Halley's Comet
Names of **historical events** and **periods**	World War II, the Middle Ages
Names of **awards** and **prizes**	Employee of the Month, the Nobel Prize
Names of **organizations** and **companies**	the United Nations, the World Health Organization, Free the Children, NoFrills, Metro
Job **titles***	Queen Elizabeth, President Ghali, Police Chief Patel, Prime Minister John A. Macdonald, Mayor Chan Lee, Dr. Smith, Mrs. Katya Petrov

* Note that a job title gets a capital letter only when it comes right before a person's name.

Canadian Grammar Practice 6 © Chalkboard Publishing

Common Nouns and Proper Nouns (continued)

1. Start all the **proper nouns** with **capital letters**. **Underline** all the **common nouns**.

   a) Is aunt wilma going to paint her house?

   b) My friend forgot that february is always the shortest month.

   c) My cousins are all helpful, but gerald and nancy are the most helpful.

   d) A nurse said that dr. lopez is moving to saskatchewan.

   e) The scientist told the audience that jupiter is the largest planet.

   f) My two favourite days of the week are saturday and sunday.

2. Start all the **proper nouns** with **capital letters**. Use the chart on the previous page to help you identify proper nouns.

   a) The peace bridge between canada and the united states was completed in 1927.

   b) The scientist marie curie won the nobel prize twice.

   c) Tourists visit niagara falls to see water rushing over steep cliffs.

   d) Some children speak french at home and english at school.

   e) A famous racehorse named northern dancer won many races.

   f) My cousin visited the cn tower on valentine's day.

   g) The planet mars has two moons, which are named deimos and phobos.

   h) Many castles were built in europe during the middle ages.

Common Nouns and Proper Nouns (continued)

The words *mom* and *dad* can be common nouns or proper nouns. When you use these words as the **names** you call these people, you are using the words as **proper nouns**, so use a capital letter.

*Examples: "Are you feeling better, **Mom**?" he asked.*
*I told **Dad** about our trip to the museum.*

If you use a **possessive adjective** (*my, your, his, her, our, their*) before *mom* or *dad*, you are not using it as a name, so it is **not** a proper noun. **Do not** use a capital letter.

*Examples: He asked his **mom** if she was feeling better.*
*I told my **dad** about our trip to the museum.*

Some job **titles** that people are given can be common nouns and proper nouns. When you use these words **right before people's names**, you are using the words as **proper nouns**, so use a capital letter.

Examples: Emperor Akihito spoke to the people of Japan about the disaster.
President Ghali will visit Queen Elizabeth in England this week.

If you use these words without the person's name, they are common nouns. They are usually used with an **article** (*a, the*) or a **possessive adjective** (*your, our, her, their, his, my*). **Do not** use a capital letter.

Examples: The president gave a speech about the local economy.
Our mayor attended the town parade with the police chief on the weekend.

3. Make all **proper nouns** start with **capital letters**. **Underline** the **common nouns**.

   a) Be sure to ask dad if we can go the royal ontario museum.

   b) Did you get your mom a mother's day card?

   c) "My dad taught me to speak spanish," mom said.

   d) "Were you and mom both born in westview hospital?" my sister asked my dad.

4. Start **proper nouns** with **capitals**. **Underline** job titles used as **common nouns**.

   a) Police chief amanda knight reported on the criminal's actions.

   b) The emperor visited the disaster zone the next day.

   c) People say the queen is very kind and well mannered.

   d) Mayor carlos sanchez held a town hall meeting today.

Canadian Grammar Practice 6 © Chalkboard Publishing

Possessive Pronouns

A **possessive pronoun** is a pronoun that shows **ownership.** Use the possessive pronouns below to replace a noun and show ownership.

mine   yours   his   hers   ours   theirs

Example: Your computer is newer than <u>my computer</u>.
            Your computer is newer than **mine**.

Possessive pronouns **do not** use an **apostrophe** to show ownership.

Rewrite each sentence. Use a **possessive pronoun** to replace the underlined words.

a) Nina ate her muffin, but I saved <u>my muffin</u> for later.

_____

b) If this bike were <u>his bike</u>, he would put new tires on it.

_____

c) Mr. Hum's house is larger than <u>our house</u>.

_____

d) Our shoes got wet, but <u>their shoes</u> stayed dry.

_____

e) I lost my ruler, so can I borrow <u>your ruler</u>?

_____

f) I have your address, but I don't have <u>her address</u>.

_____

g) Ellen found her key, but <u>my key</u> is still lost.

_____

h) I see my parents, but I don't see <u>their parents</u>.

_____

Reflexive and Intensive Pronouns

Notice the pronoun in the sentence below.

*Tim talked to **him**.*

Tim is the subject of the verb *talked*. (The subject of a verb is the person or thing doing the action.) The pronoun *him* refers to a person who is not Tim.

What if Tim is talking, and the person he is talking to is Tim? What pronoun would you use?

*Tim talked to **himself**.*

In this sentence, the pronoun *himself* refers to *Tim*. The pronoun refers to the subject of the verb *talked*.

A reflexive pronoun replaces the **subject** of a verb. Use a singular reflexive pronoun to replace a singular subject, and a plural reflexive pronoun to replace a plural subject. If the subject of the verb is *you*, decide whether *you* is used as a singular or plural pronoun.

Singular Reflexive Pronouns
myself
yourself
himself, herself, itself

Plural Reflexive Pronouns
ourselves
yourselves
themselves

Look at the examples below. The subject of each verb is underlined.

*The wet <u>dog</u> shook **itself**.* (singular subject, singular reflexive pronoun)

*The <u>children</u> looked at **themselves** in the mirror.* (plural subject, plural reflexive pronoun)

1. In each sentence, write the correct **reflexive pronoun**.

   a) We laughed at _____ in the wavy funhouse mirror.

   b) I pinched _____ to make sure I wasn't dreaming.

   c) The plant's leaves turned _____ toward the sunlight.

   d) The explorer told his crew, "You must prepare _____ for a long journey."

   e) Ari hurt _____ when he fell off his bicycle.

   f) The mouse hid _____ whenever the cat was near.

   g) Shanelle reminded _____ to return her library books.

   h) Mom told me, "You should be proud of _____."

Reflexive and Intensive Pronouns (continued)

Reflexive pronouns can also be used as **intensive pronouns**. Use intensive pronouns to add emphasis to the subject of a verb.

*Example: Sari shouldn't criticize me for what I did, since she **herself** told me to do it.*

In this sentence, *she* (Sari) is the subject of the verb *told*. Adding the intensive pronoun *herself* adds emphasis to the subject.

You can use an intensive pronoun to emphasize that the subject of the verb is doing something unusual or surprising.

*Example: Jeff hates cooking, but last night he **himself** cooked us a huge feast.*

You can also use an intensive pronoun to emphasize that the subject of the verb did something without help from others.

*Example: Reneé's parents built their garage **themselves**.*

There is an easy way to tell if a pronoun that ends with *self* or *selves* is reflexive or intensive. When you remove an **intensive** pronoun from a sentence, the sentence still makes sense and has the same meaning. This is **not** true for a **reflexive** pronoun.

*Example: Terence and Pam cleaned the kitchen **themselves**. (intensive pronoun)*

Terence and Pam cleaned the kitchen. (makes sense, same meaning)

2. Circle **R** if the bold word is a **reflexive pronoun**. Circle **I** if the bold word is an **intensive pronoun**.

a) The mayor **herself** told reporters that she would run in the next election. **R I**

b) The two burglars found **themselves** trapped on the building's rooftop. **R I**

c) He hated cleaning the oven, so he bought an oven that cleans **itself**. **R I**

d) My copy of the book is signed by the author **himself**. **R I**

e) Mrs. Jackson decided to treat **herself** to a dinner in a nice restaurant. **R I**

f) Young children often tell their parents, "I want to do it **myself**!" **R I**

g) The experts **themselves** have admitted that they might be wrong. **R I**

h) After his long hike, Joel gave **himself** a foot massage. **R I**

i) The unlucky fly got **itself** caught in the spider's web. **R I**

Canadian Grammar Practice 6 © Chalkboard Publishing   23

Indefinite Pronouns

An indefinite pronoun does **not** refer to a specific person or thing. Look at the examples below.

*Example: The firefighter said that **someone** deliberately set the fire.*
Someone is an indefinite pronoun because it does not refer to a specific **person**.

*Example: Is there **anything** you need from the grocery store?*
Anything is an indefinite pronoun because it does not refer to a specific **thing**.

*Example: **Nobody** knew who had set off the fire alarm.*
Nobody is an indefinite pronoun because it does not refer to a specific **person**.

Many indefinite pronouns begin with one of the four words shown below.

Word	Examples of Indefinite Pronouns
any	*anybody, anyone, anything*
every	*everybody, everyone, everything*
no	*nobody, no one, none, nothing*
some	*somebody, someone, something*

1. Complete each sentence by writing one of the indefinite pronouns listed above. (For some blanks, there is more than one correct answer.)

   a) It was strange that when I answered the phone, _____ was there.

   b) Marcus is such a nice person that _____ likes him.

   c) Irene looked a bit unhappy, so we wondered if _____ was wrong.

   d) I don't know _____ who doesn't like chocolate.

   e) I tried _____ to get the stain out of my favourite shirt, but

   _____ worked.

   f) Shawn was confident that _____ would find the watch he lost.

   g) I tried on three pairs of shorts, but _____ were the right size.

   h) When we moved, we had to pack _____ in boxes.

Canadian Grammar Practice 6 © Chalkboard Publishing

Indefinite Pronouns (continued)

The words below can be **indefinite pronouns**, and they can also be **adjectives**.

all	*another*	*any*	*both*	*each*	*either*	*enough*
few	*many*	*most*	*neither*	*one*	*several*	*some*

If the word describes a noun, it is being used as an **adjective**. If the word replaces a noun or pronoun, it is being used as an **indefinite pronoun**. Look at the example below.

*Example: I picked **some** tomatoes from the garden and gave **several** to Mr. Tanaka.*

In this sentence, *some* describes the noun *tomatoes*, so *some* is an **adjective.** *Several* replaces the noun *tomatoes*, so *several* is an **indefinite pronoun.**

2. Complete the second sentence in each pair.

a) Many customers came into the store, but **few** made purchases.

   Few is an indefinite pronoun replacing the noun _____.

b) She had a large collection of stamps, and **several** were quite valuable.

   Several is an indefinite pronoun replacing the noun _____.

c) Cabbages were on sale at the store, but I didn't buy **any**.

   Any is an indefinite pronoun replacing the noun _____.

d) Theo carried the eggs carefully, but **both** were cracked.

   Both is an indefinite pronoun replacing the noun _____.

e) The boy ate three cookies, then asked if he could have **another**.

   Another is an indefinite pronoun replacing the noun _____.

f) Anna liked two dresses, but **neither** were the right length.

   Neither is an indefinite pronoun replacing the noun _____.

3. **Underline** the bold words that are used as **adjectives**. **Circle** the bold words that are used as **indefinite pronouns**.

a) The teacher gave a copy of the test to **each** student.

b) **Many** people came to the talent show, but **few** stayed until the end.

c) **Both** twins were tall, but **one** was slightly taller than the other.

d) There were **several** magazines in the doctor's office, but **most** were very old.

e) He tried on two pairs of shoes, but **neither** was the right size.

f) **Some** children had the flu, but **all** felt better in a few days.

g) These two buses go north, and **either** will take you to Wellington Road.

h) **All** kittens are born with blue eyes, but **some** change colour as they grow.

i) **Enough** children signed up, so the club could start.

4. Underline the words used as adjectives. Circle the indefinite pronouns.

a) Most children did their homework, but several did not.

b) Dad made pizza for dinner, but my brother didn't eat any.

c) Strawberries are my favourite fruit, so I had some for a snack.

d) There are several ants in the kitchen, but I didn't see any get in.

e) The man brought enough trees for everyone to plant.

f) Those girls tried out for the soccer team, but one didn't make it.

g) Many boys like sports, but not all.

h) Several monkeys ate bananas, but some ate leaves instead.

i) Three birds came to the feeder, then another arrived.

Singular and Plural Indefinite Pronouns

Most indefinite pronouns are always either singular or plural.

Singular Indefinite Pronouns

Indefinite pronouns that end with **one**, **body**, or **thing** are always **singular** (except for the indefinite pronoun **none**).

Indefinite pronouns ending with **one**: *anyone, everyone, someone, one, no one*

Indefinite pronouns ending with **body**: *everybody, nobody, anybody, somebody*

Indefinite pronouns ending with **thing**: *everything, nothing, anything, something*

The indefinite pronouns below are also always **singular**.

another, each, little, either, neither

With a **singular** indefinite pronoun, use a **singular** verb (the form of the verb you use with *he, she,* or *it*).

*Examples: Everybody **is** happy that spring is finally here.*

        *No one **was** sad when winter came to an end.*

        *Nothing **makes** me happier than achieving one of my goals.*

Plural Indefinite Pronouns

The indefinite pronouns below are always **plural**.

both, few, many, others, several

With a **plural** indefinite pronoun, use a **plural** verb (the form of the verb you use with *they*).

*Examples: The police found some of the stolen jewels, but many **were** still missing.*

        *Most of the tomatoes are still green, but several **look** ripe.*

        *My parents enjoy music, and both **sing** in a choir.*

Singular and Plural Indefinite Pronouns (continued)

1. Decide whether the **bold verb** in the sentence is correct. Then **circle** the correct words in the description of the sentence. If the verb in the sample sentence is **incorrect**, cross it out and write the correct verb above it.

   a) Whenever the magician does this trick, everyone **is** amazed.

      The indefinite pronoun *everyone* is (singular plural), and the verb *is* is (singular plural), so the verb is (correct incorrect).

   b) We are trying different ways of stopping the leak, but so far nothing **work**.

      The indefinite pronoun *nothing* is (singular plural), and the verb *work* is (singular plural), so the verb is (correct incorrect).

   c) Rick borrowed two books from the library, and both **is** by the same author.

      The indefinite pronoun *both* is (singular plural), and the verb *is* is (singular plural), so the verb is (correct incorrect).

2. **Circle** the correct verb to use with each bold indefinite pronoun.

   a) The police officer watches the crowd to see if **anyone** (looks look) suspicious.

   b) Some people think the man is honest, but **others** (disagrees disagree).

   c) She wonders if **anybody** (knows know) the correct answer to the question.

   d) I like both restaurants, so **either** (is are) fine with me.

   e) Most of the students seem enthusiastic, but **several** (looks look) bored.

   f) I have two boxes, but **neither** (is are) big enough to put my computer in.

   g) There are lots of trees on my street, and **many** (was were) damaged in the storm.

   h) I packed two large suitcases, and **each** (weighs weigh) more than 40 pounds.

   i) **Little** (is are) known about the newly discovered creature.

   j) Many people want to become famous, but **few** (succeeds succeed).

   k) One student has finished the test, and **another** (is are) almost finished.

Pronouns and Antecedents

An **antecedent** is the word or words that a pronoun refers to. Look at the examples below.

Example: (The kittens) were hungry, so Gail fed <u>them</u>.

The pronoun *them* replaces *the kittens*. *The kittens* is the **antecedent** of the pronoun *them*.

Example: (The boys) had walked all day, so <u>they</u> wanted to rest.

The pronoun *they* replaces *the boys*. *The boys* is the **antecedent** of the pronoun *they*.

1. **Circle** the antecedent of each underlined pronoun. **Draw an arrow** from each underlined pronoun to its antecedent.

a) Freddy hit the puck, and <u>it</u> went into the net.

b) Gemma is pleased that <u>she</u> found a solution to the problem.

c) Please fold the clothes and put <u>them</u> away.

d) Diego was hungry, so I gave <u>him</u> some grapes.

e) I enjoyed the book, and my sister liked <u>it</u> even more than I did.

f) Two bears came to our tent, but <u>they</u> didn't try to get inside.

g) Tia found a quarter, and <u>she</u> put <u>it</u> in her pocket.

h) Mom bought John a sweater, but <u>it</u> didn't fit <u>him</u>.

One pronoun can replace **two or more nouns**.

Example: (The dog and the cat) get along well, and <u>they</u> often play together.
The antecedent of the pronoun *they* is *the dog and the cat*.

i) If Frank, Tony, and Leah aren't busy, <u>they</u> might want to come over.

j) I borrowed a book and a video from the library, and I returned <u>them</u> a week later.

k) Grapes, apples, and oranges are nutritious, so Mom always buys <u>them</u>.

l) The finches and sparrows are hungry, so <u>they</u> are always at the bird feeder.

m) I asked my brother and my sister, "Could <u>you</u> please make less noise?"

Pronouns and Antecedents (continued)

An antecedent can contain one or more nouns **and** a pronoun, or **more than one** pronoun. Look at the examples below.

Example: Dad and I got wet washing the car, so <u>we</u> had to change our clothes.
The antecedent of the pronoun *we* is *Dad and I. Dad* is a noun, and *I* is a pronoun.

Example: He and I like the same sports, so <u>we</u> often watch games together.
The antecedent of the pronoun *we* is *He and I. He* and *I* are both pronouns.

2. **Circle** the antecedent of each underlined pronoun. **Draw an arrow** from each underlined pronoun to its antecedent.

a) Raj and I were thirsty, so <u>we</u> got some juice from the refrigerator.

b) He and the twins are on the same swim team, so <u>they</u> know each other well.

c) Tara, Joan, and I were bored, so Dad took <u>us</u> to the amusement park.

d) She and I met two years ago, and <u>we</u> have become good friends.

e) Dominic found a hat and a scarf, so <u>he</u> took <u>them</u> to the lost-and-found.

f) Frogs and turtles live in this pond, and <u>they</u> burrow into the muddy bottom for winter.

g) He and she went to the library, and <u>they</u> came home with three books each.

h) Mia found a loonie on the sidewalk, and <u>she</u> bought a juice with <u>it</u>.

i) The puppies in the box were crying, so their mother came and fed <u>them</u>.

j) The police chased the criminals, then <u>they</u> caught and arrested <u>them</u>.

k) Grandma gave Timmy and I two kisses each, and <u>we</u> gave two back to <u>her</u>.

l) Sunshine is wonderful because <u>it</u> warms the earth and makes plants grow.

Pronouns and Antecedents (continued)

The antecedent of a pronoun can appear in a **previous sentence**.

Example: Aunt Ruth *is very generous.* She *gives money to several charities.*
Aunt Ruth *is the antecedent of the pronoun* She*.*

3. **Circle** the antecedent of each underlined pronoun. **Draw an arrow** from each underlined pronoun to its antecedent.

   a) The doctor gave me some medicine. I have to take <u>it</u> three times a day.

   b) Snow fell for three days. By the third day, <u>it</u> was two feet deep.

   c) My cousins are coming to stay for four days. We'll meet <u>them</u> at the airport.

   d) Her grandparents love animals. <u>They</u> have a cat, and <u>it</u> stares hungrily at their pet canary.

   e) Michelle lent Lucy and me two videos. <u>She</u> asked <u>us</u> to return <u>them</u> by Thursday.

   f) Do you want to go swimming with me? <u>We</u> could meet at the community centre.

4. **Circle** the antecedent. **Underline** the pronoun. **Draw an arrow** from each pronoun to its antecedent.

   a) Frank walked to school with Annie. He told jokes to make her laugh.

   b) The monkeys are scared of me and Kerry. They scurry up the tree and screech at us.

   c) The teacher said I did well on the spelling test. She gave me a gold star.

   d) The man delivered a package for my sister and me. We were excited to open it.

   e) Jack, Rita, and I went to the movies with Lee. We met him at the theatre.

   f) Furry caterpillars are all over that tree. They are eating all the leaves off it.

   g) My cousins and my family have a barbecue with fireworks every July 1. We have lots of fun!

   h) Lily and Mickey went swimming in the lake. They said it was very cold.

   i) Tony bought a bag of marbles. He opened it and sorted them into groups.

Identifying Unclear Antecedents

Pronouns and possessive adjectives have antecedents.

Example: <u>Mrs. Gomez</u> *will take a vacation if* **she** *can get time off work.*

In this sentence, *Mrs. Gomez* is the antecedent of the pronoun *she*.

Example: <u>Eddie</u> *always rides* **his** *bike to school.*

In this sentence, *Eddie* is the antecedent of the possessive adjective *his*.

Sentences become confusing when the antecedent of a pronoun or possessive adjective is not clear to readers.

Example: Frank told Tom that **his** *new computer is amazing.*

Does Frank have a new computer that is amazing, or does Tom? The sentence is confusing because it is not clear whether *Frank* or *Tom* is the antecedent of *his*.

Example: Valerie saw Kim when **she** *was walking to the store.*

Which girl was walking to the store? The sentence is confusing because it is not clear whether *Valerie* or *Kim* is the antecedent of *she*.

Does the sentence contain a pronoun or possessive adjective with an **unclear antecedent**? Circle **Yes** or **No**. If you answer **Yes**,

• circle the pronoun or possessive adjective with an unclear antecedent
• underline the two possible antecedents of the pronoun you circled.

a) Mr. Jones bought a kitten, and he named it Fluffy. **Yes No**

b) After the woman yelled at Kate, she felt terrible. **Yes No**

c) I took the card out of the envelope and put it in the trash. **Yes No**

d) Jim told Dad that a button fell off his shirt. **Yes No**

e) There was lightning during the storms, and we loved watching it. **Yes No**

f) Lisa argued with Victoria, but later she apologized. **Yes No**

g) The girls told their brother that he shouldn't tease them. **Yes No**

h) Leo asked his uncle if he is taller than Sami. **Yes No**

Correcting Unclear Antecedents

Here are three strategies for correcting unclear antecedents.

1. Repeat the noun instead of using a pronoun or possessive adjective.

2. Revise the sentence by finding a different way to communicate the idea.

3. If the sentence is about what one person said to another, try using dialogue.

Example 1

Unclear antecedent: *Frank told Tom that his new computer is amazing.*
(The writer meant that Frank's new computer is amazing.)

Repeat the noun: *Frank told Tom that Frank's new computer is amazing.*

Revise the sentence: *Frank has a new computer, and he told Tom it is amazing.*

Use dialogue: *Frank told Tom, "My new computer is amazing."*

Example 2

Unclear antecedent: *Valerie saw Kim when she was walking to the store.*
(The writer meant that Valerie was walking to the store.)

Repeat the noun: *Valerie saw Kim when Valerie was walking to the store.*

Revise the sentence: *Valerie was walking to the store when she saw Kim.*

(The sentence is not about what one person said to another, so the strategy of using dialogue doesn't work.)

1. **Rewrite** each sentence. (Do not rewrite the sentences in brackets.) Use the strategy of **repeating a noun** to avoid an unclear antecedent.

   a) The last scene in the movie was great, so I watched it again and again.
      (The writer watched the last scene again and again.)

   _____

   _____

   b) Theo didn't stay long at Ralph's house because his aunt was coming to visit.
      (The aunt is Ralph's relative.)

   _____

   _____

Correcting Unclear Antecedents (continued)

2. **Rewrite** each sentence. To avoid an unclear antecedent, use the strategy of **revising the sentence**, using a different way of communicating the idea. (**Do not** repeat a noun.)

a) Rani missed Sue while she was away. (Rani was away.)

_____

_____

b) Ahmed knew the cat wanted to eat his goldfish, so he watched it carefully. (Ahmed watched the cat.)

_____

_____

c) After the truck hit the bus, it had a flat tire. (The bus did not have a flat tire.)

_____

d) When Mom finally saw her sister again, she cried tears of joy. (The tears were Mom's.)

_____

_____

e) Renata played a video game with Wendy because she was bored. (Wendy was bored.)

_____

_____

f) Marc shared a pizza with Pierre and he ate three slices. (Pierre ate 3 slices.)

_____

_____

Correcting Unclear Antecedents (continued)

3. **Rewrite** each sentence. To avoid an unclear antecedent, **use dialogue**.

a) Mr. Fong told Mr. Prince that he needed a vacation. (Mr. Prince needed a vacation.)

_____

_____

b) The students told their teachers that they always work hard. (The students always work hard.)

_____

_____

c) Mary told Whiskers she is always neat and clean. (Whiskers is clean.)

_____

_____

d) Tim told Mitch he is going to eat hotdogs for lunch. (Tim will eat hotdogs.)

_____

_____

e) The girl told her mother she needs to buy the pretty green dress. (The girl needs the dress.)

_____

_____

f) Dad told Rajesh he can hike to the top of the hill easily. (Rajesh can hike to the top.)

_____

_____

Avoiding Pairs of Pronouns

If a singular antecedent refers to a person and the person could be male or female, you can use one of the following pairs of pronouns: *he or she, she or he, him or her, her or him.*

Some people find that using these pairs of pronouns sounds awkward, especially if they occur more than once in a paragraph. To avoid using pairs of pronouns, some people use *they* or *them* when the antecedent is singular.

*Examples: If a <u>customer</u> is not satisfied, **they** should speak to the manager.*
*Julie could call a <u>friend</u> and ask **them** to play chess with her.*

The pronouns *they* and *them* are plural. In the example sentences above, these plural pronouns are used with singular antecedents. The pronouns and antecedents do not agree in number. Some people say it is acceptable to use **they** and **them** in sentences like the ones above. Other people disagree.

If you want to avoid using pairs of pronouns, and you don't want to use a plural pronoun with a singular antecedent, there are two strategies you can try.

Strategy 1: Make the sentence plural.

Look at the example below.

Singular: *If a <u>customer</u> is not satisfied, **he or she** should speak to the manager.*
Plural: *If <u>customers</u> are not satisfied, **they** should speak to the manager.*

Making the sentence plural works for the example above. However, look at the example below.

Singular: *Julie could call a <u>friend</u> and ask **him or her** to play a game of chess with her.*
Plural: *Julie could call some <u>friends</u> and ask **them** to play a game of chess with her.*

Making the sentence plural doesn't work in this case. Chess is a game for two people, so Julie needs only one friend to play chess with her.

Strategy 2: Rewrite the sentence to avoid the problem pronoun.

When making a sentence plural doesn't work, see if you can rewrite the sentence to express the idea in a way that avoids the pronoun problem.

Original: *Julie could call a <u>friend</u> and ask **him or her** to play a game of chess with her.*
Rewritten: *Julie could find out if a friend will play a game of chess with her.*

Avoiding Pairs of Pronouns (continued)

1. Make each sentence **plural** to avoid using pairs of pronouns (*he or she, she or he, him or her, her or him*).

   a) When a student has the flu, she or he should stay home from school.

   _____

   _____

   b) A passenger should take care not to leave his or her luggage on the train.

   _____

   _____

   c) If you see a person who looks lost, ask him or her if he or she needs directions.

   _____

   _____

   d) When a guest is leaving, we thank him or her for staying at our hotel.

   _____

   _____

2. Rewrite each sentence to **avoid** using pairs of pronouns. (Making the sentence plural **does not** work with these sentences.)

   a) The car has room for one more person, so I will ask a friend if he or she wants to come with us.

   _____

   _____

   b) We'll hire one new employee, and the manager will train her or him.

   _____

   _____

Nouns and Pronouns Review Quiz

1. Change the first letter of **proper nouns** into a capital letter.

   a) During our trip to montreal last july, we ate at a french restaurant.

   b) As we stood on the brooklyn bridge in new york city, halley's comet crossed the sky.

   c) The battle of hastings was fought in england during the middle ages.

2. At the end of each sentence, write the **possessive pronoun** that could be used to replace the underlined words.

   a) I've met your parents, but you haven't met <u>my parents</u>. _____

   b) Her joke was funny, but <u>his joke</u> wasn't funny at all. _____

   c) We have visited their home, and next week they will visit <u>our home</u>. _____

   d) My bike has a flat tire, so may I borrow <u>your bike</u>? _____

3. Complete each sentence by writing the correct **reflexive pronoun**.

   a) Sometimes when I am alone, I talk to _____.

   b) We had many mosquito bites, so we covered _____ with anti-itch cream.

   c) The heater will turn _____ off when the room is warm enough.

   d) Students, you must prepare _____ for the test by studying hard.

4. Circle *R* if the underlined word is a **reflexive pronoun**. Circle *I* if the underlined word is an **intensive pronoun**.

   a) Isabella told <u>herself</u> to stay calm and not get upset. *I* *R*

   b) The police chief <u>himself</u> interviewed the suspect. *I* *R*

   c) I'm glad you like the story because I wrote it <u>myself</u>. *I* *R*

   d) The team members congratulated <u>themselves</u> on their victory. *I* *R*

   e) If we can't find a good play to perform, we'll write a play <u>ourselves</u>. *I* *R*

Canadian Grammar Practice 6 © Chalkboard Publishing

5. **Underline** the **indefinite pronouns** in the sentences below. (Remember that some words can be indefinite pronouns or adjectives.) Then **circle** the correct verb.

   a) Everybody in my family likes carrots, but no one (like likes) beets.

   b) If you need help with anything, someone (is are) available to help you.

   c) The twins enjoy knitting sweaters, and both (has have) made several.

   d) Many students came to the bake sale, but few (is are) still here.

6. Circle the **antecedent** of the bold pronoun or pronouns in each sentence.

   a) She took the books to the shelves and put **them** back where **they** belonged.

   b) Angelo saw a deer near the river, but **it** quickly ran away.

   c) Mrs. Ling bought bananas for the children, but **they** were still green.

   d) Lucy, Jerry, and I wanted to go see a movie, but **we** didn't have any money.

7. Does the sentence need to be revised because one or more pronouns or possessive adjectives have **unclear antecedents**? Circle *Yes* or *No*.

   a) Yolanda asked her mom if she looked like her grandmother. *Yes   No*

   b) A commercial came on TV, so I changed the channel until it was over. *Yes   No*

   c) The baseball hit a tree, and then it rolled under a car. *Yes   No*

   d) Gianni told his dad that he liked his new shirt. *Yes   No*

8. Revise the sentence below to correct the unclear antecedent. The revised sentence should communicate the meaning in brackets

   Jane couldn't play catch with Denise because she was busy. (Jane was busy.)

   _____

   _____

Pronoun–Antecedent Agreement: Number

A pronoun and its antecedent must "agree" with each other. This means that a pronoun and its antecedent must be the same in certain ways. This page looks at the first rule for making pronouns and antecedents agree.

Rule: A pronoun and its antecedent must agree in number.

If the antecedent is singular, use a singular pronoun. If the antecedent is plural, use a plural pronoun.

Singular Pronouns	**Plural Pronouns**
I, me	*we, us*
you	*you*
he, him, she, her, it	*they, them*

*Example: Amanda dropped her **glove**, so she picked **it** up.*

Glove is the antecedent of the pronoun *it*. *Glove* is a **singular** noun, and *it* is a **singular** pronoun. The pronoun and its antecedent are **both** singular, so they agree in **number**.

*Example: Amanda dropped her **gloves**, so she picked **them** up.*

In this sentence, the antecedent *gloves* is a **plural** noun, and *them* is a **plural** pronoun. The pronoun and its antecedent are **both** plural, so they agree in **number**.

*Example: **Incorrect:** Amanda dropped her **glove**, so she picked **them** up.*

In this sentence, the antecedent *glove* is a **singular** noun, and the pronoun *them* is **plural**.

The pronoun and its antecedent **do not** agree in **number**, so the pronoun is incorrect. The singular pronoun *it* should be used to make the pronoun and its antecedent agree in number.

Notice that the pronoun **you** can be either **singular or plural**.

*Example: **Singular:** Young **man**, could **you** please help me?*

In this sentence, *man* is the antecedent of the pronoun *you*. *Man* is singular, and *you* is used as a singular pronoun. The pronoun and antecedent are **both** singular, so they agree in **number**.

*Example: **Plural: Students**, **you** must hand in your reports by next Monday.*

In this sentence, *students* is the antecedent of the pronoun *you*. *Students* is plural, and *you* is used as a plural pronoun. The pronoun and antecedent are **both** plural, so they agree in **number**.

Canadian Grammar Practice 6 © Chalkboard Publishing

Pronoun–Antecedent Agreement: Number (continued)

1. **Circle** the correct choices in the description of each sample sentence.

   a) We thought our daughters might get bored, but she loved the movie.

   The pronoun *she* is (singular plural), and the antecedent *daughters* is (singular plural). The pronoun and antecedent (do do not) agree in number.

   b) My friends, I am so happy you could be here today.

   The pronoun *you* is (singular plural), and the antecedent *friends* is (singular plural). The pronoun and antecedent (do do not) agree in number.

   c) If I made some errors, I will be sure to correct it.

   The pronoun *it* is (singular plural), and the antecedent *errors* is (singular plural). The pronoun and antecedent (do do not) agree in number.

2. In two of the sentences in Question 1, the pronouns and their antecedents **do not** agree in number. **Rewrite** those sentences below, using the correct pronoun.

   Sentence: _____

   _____

   Sentence: _____

   _____

3. **Circle** the correct pronoun to make the pronoun and its antecedent **agree in number**.

   a) Tornadoes are very powerful, and (it they) can destroy a house in seconds.

   b) If Wanda has a sore muscle, she could try gently stretching (it them).

   c) I asked my friend to return the books, and I hope (she they) will.

   d) He used to know the words to that song, but he can't remember (it them) now.

   e) When people are nervous about something, (he they) should try to stay calm.

   f) When deer come into our yard, we watch (it them) through the window.

Compound Antecedents: Number Agreement

A **compound antecedent** is made up of two or more words joined by **and** or **or**.

When the words are joined by **and**, the antecedent is **plural**, so use a **plural pronoun**.

Example: <u>Priya **and** I</u> were hot, so **we** went for a swim in the lake.

Priya and I is a **plural** antecedent, so the **plural** pronoun *we* creates agreement in number.

When the words in a compound antecedent are joined by **or**, look at the nouns in the antecedent to see which noun is **closest** to the pronoun. If that noun is **singular**, use a **singular pronoun**.

Example: When you eat <u>an apple **or** a pear</u>, wash **it** well first.

The antecedent is *an apple or a pear. Pear* is the noun closest to the pronoun, and *pear* is **singular,** so the **singular** pronoun *it* is required.

If the noun that is closest to the pronoun is **plural**, use a **plural pronoun**.

Example: When you eat <u>an apple **or** grapes</u>, wash **them** well first.

The antecedent is *an apple or grapes. Grapes* is the noun closest to the pronoun, and *grapes* is **plural**, so the **plural** pronoun *them* is required.

In each sentence, **underline** the compound antecedent. Then **circle** the correct pronoun.

a) If you see Liz or Anna, tell (her them) that I can't come to the party.

b) Gino and Sal will probably come, but (he they) might be late.

c) Terry, Cara, and I live close to the park, so (I we) often play soccer there.

d) If Miguel or Tony will cut the grass, Mrs. Ramirez will pay (him them).

e) When my brothers and my dad get home, I'll make (him them) dinner.

f) If you are shopping for a shirt or boots, try (it them) on first.

g) Take gloves or mittens with you, so you can wear (it them) if your hands are cold.

h) If you find Lena's earrings or bracelet, take (it them) to the lost-and-found.

i) The kittens and their mother were scared, so (it they) hid under the bed.

j) The teacher or the students might help us, if we ask (her them) nicely.

Pronoun–Antecedent Agreement: Gender

A pronoun and its antecedent must "agree" with each other. This means that a pronoun and its antecedent must be the same in certain ways. This page looks at the second rule for making pronouns and antecedents agree.

Rule: A pronoun and its antecedent must agree in gender.

Nouns come in three genders: **masculine**, **feminine**, and **neuter**. Neuter means "neither masculine nor feminine." Most nouns are neuter, unless they refer to a male or female person or animal.

Examples: ***masculine nouns:*** *father, son, uncle, boy, king, rooster*
   feminine nouns: *mother, daughter, aunt, girl, queen, hen*
   neuter nouns: *car, sky, pillow, bird, house, mountain*

When the antecedent is a **singular masculine noun**, use the singular masculine pronoun **he** or **him** to make the pronoun and antecedent agree in gender. When the antecedent is a **singular feminine noun**, use the singular feminine pronoun **she** or **her** to make the pronoun and antecedent agree in gender.

Examples: <u>Peter</u> *had run all the way to school, so* **he** *was out of breath.*
   When my <u>aunt</u> was in the hospital, we often went to visit **her***.*

When the antecedent is a **singular neuter noun** that does not refer to a person, use the singular neuter pronoun **it** to make the pronoun and antecedent agree in gender.

Example: The person who borrowed my <u>stapler</u> has not returned **it***.*

When the antecedent is **plural**, use the plural pronoun **they** or **them**. For a plural noun, it does not matter if the noun is masculine, feminine, or neuter.

Examples: When my <u>brothers</u> are bored, **they** *play chess.*
   I ran into <u>Tina and Catherine</u>, so I chatted with **them** *for a while.*
   I didn't like the last two <u>paragraphs</u> of my report, so I rewrote **them***.*

Some neuter nouns refer to a person. If you know whether the person is male or female, use the appropriate masculine or feminine pronoun.

Examples: I asked my <u>teacher</u> if **he** *would read my story.*
   My <u>friend</u> said **she** *missed me while I was away.*

If the person could be male or female, use masculine *and* feminine pronouns: ***he or she*** *or* ***she or he, him or her*** *or* ***her or him.***

Examples: I don't know who will be my <u>teacher</u> next year, but I hope I like ***him or her***.
   Ask a <u>salesperson</u> if ***she or he*** *can explain how to use the product.*

Pronoun–Antecedent Agreement: Gender (continued)

Underline the antecedent and **write** the correct pronoun or pronouns. Then **circle** the correct choices in the sentence describing the antecedent.

a) The plant was wilting, so Gerard watered _____.

   The antecedent is (masculine feminine neuter) and (singular plural).

b) When a police officer arrives, tell _____ what you saw.

   The antecedent is (masculine feminine neuter) and (singular plural).

c) The children laughed as _____ chased after the squirrel.

   The antecedent is (masculine feminine neuter) and (singular plural).

d) I know your daughter, but _____ is not in my class.

   The antecedent is (masculine feminine neuter) and (singular plural).

e) On Grandpa's birthday, _____ likes to eat cake and ice cream.

   The antecedent is (masculine feminine neuter) and (singular plural).

f) The story is about a princess and the prince who wanted to marry _____.

   The antecedent is (masculine feminine neuter) and (singular plural).

g) When a new mayor is elected, _____ will make a speech.

   The antecedent is (masculine feminine neuter) and (singular plural).

h) If the boys come home from school soon, _____ can watch a video while I make dinner.

   The antecedent is (masculine feminine neuter) and (singular plural).

i) If you have an older sibling, you can ask _____ to help you with your homework.

   The antecedent is (masculine feminine neuter) and (singular plural).

Number and Gender Agreement Review Quiz

1. **Circle** the correct choices in the description of each sample sentence.

   a) The night sky was full of clouds, and it covered most of the stars.

   The pronoun *it* is (singular plural), and the antecedent *clouds* is
   (singular plural). The pronoun and antecedent (do do not) agree in number.

   b) She wore two rings on her finger, and they glittered in the bright sunlight.

   The pronoun *they* is (singular plural), and the antecedent *rings* is
   (singular plural). The pronoun and antecedent (do do not) agree in number.

2. **Circle** the correct pronoun and then identify its **antecedent**.

   a) Orli wrote comments on my report, and I agreed with most of (it them).

   The antecedent of the pronoun I circled is _____.

   b) Mrs. Gupta and her son were sick, but (she they) are feeling better now.

   The antecedent of the pronoun I circled is _____.

   c) I like my cousins, but one of (him them) sometimes teases me.

   The antecedent of the pronoun I circled is _____.

   d) The child was making too much noise, so I asked (her them) to be quiet.

   The antecedent of the pronoun I circled is _____.

   e) If you wash your sheets or pillowcase, hang (it them) outside to dry.

   The antecedent of the pronoun I circled is _____.

   f) If Franco and Kyle come over, maybe (he they) can stay for supper.

   The antecedent of the pronoun I circled is _____.

   g) If you see Irene or her parents, please tell (her them) that I am feeling better.

   The antecedent of the pronoun I circled is _____.

Number and Gender Agreement Review Quiz (continued)

3. **Underline** the antecedent and **write** the correct pronoun, pronouns, or possessive adjective.

   a) The submarine surprised the sailors as _____ came to the ocean's surface.

   b) I am going to ask a doctor why _____ chose that profession.

   c) Mr. Peters bought his daughter a new bike for _____ birthday.

   d) My sisters are very proud of _____ rock collection.

   e) Some students asked a parent if _____ could help with the bake sale.

4. Make each sentence **plural** to avoid using pairs of pronouns (*he or she, she or he, him or her, her or him*).

   a) When a student is not feeling well, she or he should see the school nurse.

   _____

   b) A voter must cast his or her vote before 9:00 p.m. on Thursday.

   _____

5. Rewrite each sentence to **avoid** using pairs of pronouns. (Making the sentence plural **does not** work with these sentences.)

   a) I need someone to play tennis with on Saturday, so I will ask a friend if she or he wants to play.

   _____

   _____

   b) After the new mayor is elected, a reporter will interview him or her.

   _____

   _____

Adjective or Noun?

Nouns are often used as adjectives. Compare the examples below.

*Example: The shirt I'm wearing is made of **cotton**.*
In this sentence, *cotton* is a noun.

*Example: I'm wearing a **cotton** shirt today.*
In this sentence, *cotton* is used as an adjective describing the noun *shirt*.

1. Circle **ADJ** if the bold word is used as an **adjective**. Circle **N** if the bold word is used as a **noun**.

   a) We can't play **baseball** without a bat. *ADJ N*

   b) She swung the **baseball** bat as hard as she could. *ADJ N*

   c) There was a report about the tornado on the **evening** news. *ADJ N*

   d) We saw a report about the tornado on the news this **evening**. *ADJ N*

2. In each sentence, underline any **nouns** that are used as **adjectives**.

   a) Pieces of a broken coffee mug lay on the kitchen floor.

   b) Air pollution is often a problem during hot, humid summer weather.

   c) I ate delicious food at a nearby restaurant, and then I went home for a short nap.

   d) The free exhibition at the art gallery featured new paintings by local artists.

   e) The movie is a love story about young people who encounter difficult challenges.

   f) We browsed in the gift shop and had an interesting chat with the store manager.

   g) If I don't become a basketball player, I might become a sports broadcaster.

   h) When I crave something sweet, I eat seedless grapes instead of a chocolate bar.

   i) The bathroom sink in our hotel room was a bowl made of clear glass.

   j) The abandoned house is an unsafe place for neighbourhood children to play.

Adjective or Noun? (continued)

Adjectives can be used as nouns to name a person or group of people. Compare the examples below.

*Example: Four **injured** people were taken to hospital after the accident.*

In this sentence, *injured* is an adjective describing the noun *people*.

*Example: Ambulances took the **injured** for treatment at Westview Hospital.*

In this sentence, *injured* is used as a noun to name the group of people who were hurt. Notice that *the* appears before an adjective used as a noun to name a group of people.

3. Circle **ADJ** if the bold word is used as an **adjective**. Circle **N** if the bold word is used as a **noun**.

   a) I helped raise money to build a new shelter for the **homeless**. *ADJ N*

   b) It is sad to see so many **homeless** people in large cities. *ADJ N*

   c) Stan offered to help his **elderly** neighbour by cutting her grass. *ADJ N*

   d) The **elderly** were advised to stay indoors during extremely hot weather. *ADJ N*

4. **Underline** all the nouns used as adjectives. **Circle** all the adjectives used as nouns.

   a) She donated most of her lottery prize to charities that help the poor and the sick.

   b) The young doctor clearly explained how blood vessels carry blood to all body parts.

   c) Battles between the English and the French have occurred throughout history.

   d) At the Italian restaurant, we ate bread rolls and pasta with meatless spaghetti sauce.

   e) On my computer screen, I opened the desktop folder where I keep family photos.

   f) The purpose of the government program is to help the unemployed find work.

   g) A popular saying tells us that "only the strong survive."

   h) A bicycle helmet should be worn by all cyclists to prevent head injuries.

   i) The winners held a victory party, and the losers discussed why they lost the game.

What Can Adverbs Describe?

An Adverb Can Describe a Verb

An adverb can answer one of the following questions about a verb:
When? Where? How? How often? How much?

In the examples below, the adverb is in bold and the verb the adverb describes is underlined.

Question	Example
When?	***Yesterday*** we <u>celebrated</u> my grandparents' wedding anniversary.
Where?	The frightened bird <u>flew</u> ***away***.
How?	The students <u>talked</u> ***quietly*** among themselves.
How often?	Mrs. Sanchez ***often*** <u>reads</u> the newspaper after dinner.
How much?	We ***strongly*** <u>disagreed</u> with the speaker's opinions.

An Adverb Can Describe an Adjective

An adverb that describes an adjective often answers the question "To what degree?" (The question "To what degree?" is similar to the question "How much?") In the examples below, the adverb is in bold and the adjective the adverb describes is underlined.

*We were **very** <u>tired</u> after our long journey.*

*The scientists are **quite** <u>surprised</u> with the results of the experiment.*

*The children became **more** <u>helpful</u> to their mother after she broke her leg.*

The words *tired*, *surprised*, and *helpful* are all adjectives. The bold adverb in each sentence is describing an adjective.

An Adverb Can Describe Another Adverb

In the examples below, two adverbs are underlined. The adverb in bold is describing the other underlined adverb.

*Leon is **<u>almost</u>** <u>always</u> late for school.*

*When the fire alarm rang, we walked **<u>very</u>** <u>quickly</u> out of the building.*

*Our soccer team played **<u>extremely</u>** <u>well</u> in the last game.*

The words *always*, *quickly*, and *well* are all adverbs. Notice how each bold adverb describes the underlined adverb that is not bold.

What Can Adverbs Describe?

1. **Circle** the adverb that describes a **verb**. **Underline** the verb that the adverb describes.

    a) Let's leave now so we can avoid rush-hour traffic.

    b) If you are hungry, we can stop here for lunch.

    c) Mr. Chan sometimes considers moving to Bristish Columbia.

    d) Karen always splashes in puddles when it rains.

    e) The children giggled loudly when the dog begged for a treat.

    f) Tim and Jenny skipped happily to the park to play on the swings.

    g) She talked so quickly, I could barely understand a word she said.

    h) When the fire alarm sounds, we walk quickly and quietly outside.

    i) We found a dripping wet cat meowing sadly in our backyard.

    j) We slowly sipped hot chocolate beside the flickering fire in the cottage.

2. **Circle** the adverb that describes an **adjective**. **Underline** the adjective that the adverb describes.

    a) Selena was rather disappointed when her poem did not win the poetry contest.

    b) It was extremely cold outside, so we stayed indoors.

    c) The last problem on the math test was very difficult.

    d) We bought the least expensive jam we could find at the store.

    e) Tim followed the instructions very carefully.

    f) Alicia drew the most colourful picture in class.

    g) The neighbour's dog is always friendly toward me and my sister.

    h) I didn't pass my last spelling test, so I need to study this time.

    i) My father and I walked through the light golden grasses in the meadow.

    j) The fluffy soft kitten purred loudly when the girl patted her.

    k) The incredibly strong man pulled a small car by a chain.

What Can Adverbs Describe? (continued)

3. **Circle** the adverb that describes another **adverb**. **Underline** the adverb that is described by the adverb you circled.

   a) Ralph played his piece nearly perfectly at the piano recital.

   b) I thought she was tired because she walked unusually slowly.

   c) You can quite easily clean that pot if you soak it in hot water first.

   d) The guests were dressed very formally for the mayor's banquet.

   e) The robin almost always perched outside my window in the morning.

   f) Tami ate spaghetti but she never really liked the taste of it.

   g) High in the mountains, it frequently snows heavily.

   h) Jack ran around the corner extremely quickly and scared the dog.

   i) The birds sang very happily as the sun rose this morning.

4. What is the **bold adverb** describing? Circle *V* for a verb, *ADJ* for an adjective, or *ADV* for an adverb.

   a) The teacher asked John to speak louder because he talks **too** softly.
   V ADJ ADV

   b) The children were sad to see that the cookie jar was **completely** empty.
   V ADJ ADV

   c) The dog ate her food **so** quickly that we knew she must be very hungry.
   V ADJ ADV

   d) We **never** expected to see such high temperatures in early spring.
   V ADJ ADV

   e) Tori was **absolutely** certain that she had done well on the science quiz.
   V ADJ ADV

Adjective or Adverb?

Some words can be used as an adjective or an adverb. Look at the examples below.

*Example 1: We publish our newsletter **weekly**.*
*Yesterday, I made my **weekly** trip to the grocery store.*

In the first sentence, *weekly* is an adverb describing the verb *publish*. In the second sentence, *weekly* is an adjective describing the noun *trip*.

*Example 2: Thomas is the **most** reliable person I know.*
***Most** people feel that there are too many commercials on TV.*

In the first sentence, *most* is an adverb describing the adjective *reliable*. (Remember that adverbs can describe verbs, adjectives, and other adverbs.) In the second sentence, *most* is an adjective describing the noun *people*.

Below are more words that can be used as an adjective or an adverb.

early late hard high fast low

Decide whether the underlined word is used as an **adjective** or **adverb**. Then **complete** the next sentence.

Example: This paper is suitable for use in <u>most</u> printers.
Most is an <u>adjective</u> describing the <u>noun printers.</u>

a) Lorenza gave the <u>most</u> convincing reasons to support her opinion.

  Most is an _____ describing the _____.

b) The panther hunched <u>low</u> to the ground as it stalked its prey.

  Low is an _____ describing the _____.

c) You'll need to take an <u>early</u> train if you want to arrive by noon.

  Early is an _____ describing the _____.

Adjective or Adverb? (continued)

d) Be sure to aim <u>high</u> when you set goals for yourself.

High is an _____ describing the _____.

e) Sometimes a <u>fast</u> solution to a problem is not the best solution.

Fast is an _____ describing the _____.

f) We rarely have such <u>low</u> temperatures in July.

Low is an _____ describing the _____.

g) She'll need to walk <u>fast</u> if she wants to catch up with them.

Fast is an _____ describing the _____.

h) Hal made it a habit to always arrive <u>early</u> for appointments.

Early is an _____ describing the _____.

i) It was <u>hard</u> work to complete our project by the deadline.

Hard is an _____ describing the _____.

j) The helicopter flew <u>high</u> over the treetops.

High is an _____ describing the _____.

k) I usually arrive on time, but today the bus was <u>late</u>.

Late is an _____ describing the _____.

l) The skateboarder hit the ground <u>hard</u> when he fell.

Hard is an _____ describing the _____.

m) The dog always hides when it is time for his <u>weekly</u> bath.

Weekly is an _____ describing the _____.

n) Mrs. Grimaldi is the <u>most</u> intelligent person I know.

Most is an _____ describing the _____.

Adjectives and Adverbs Review Quiz

1. Circle **ADJ** if the bold word is used as an **adjective**. Circle **N** if the bold word is used as a **noun**.

   a) Members of the team gathered on the **football** field. *ADJ N*

   b) I kicked the **football** right through the goalposts. *ADJ N*

   c) In the middle of her speech, someone's **telephone** rang. *ADJ N*

   d) A group of birds sat on the **telephone** wire outside my window. *ADJ N*

   e) We sent Kenny a **sympathy** card when his grandfather died. *ADJ N*

   f) We should all feel **sympathy** for the victims of the earthquake. *ADJ N*

   g) That black <u>race</u> horse almost always finishes first. *ADJ N*

   h) Nick entered the <u>race</u> for class president and won by a landslide. *ADJ N*

2. In each sentence, underline any **nouns** that are used as **adjectives**.

   a) Tamara carefully wiped the fingerprints off the computer screen.

   b) You can reheat the beef stew in a toaster oven.

   c) It was a lovely day, so we ate a late lunch at a sidewalk café.

   d) I drink chocolate milk or apple juice when I get thirsty.

   e) At the hardware store, we bought light bulbs and a measuring tape.

   f) Jesse hung his coat on the metal hanger in the hall closet.

   g) Amy threw a tennis ball against the stone wall.

   h) The twins used plastic buckets to make the perfect sand castle.

   i) Beautiful organ music floated through the open church doors.

3. Circle **ADJ** if the bold word is used as an **adjective**. Circle **N** if the bold word is used as a **noun**.

a) This parking spot is reserved for the **disabled**. *ADJ N*

b) A **disabled** veteran told the audience of his experiences as a soldier. *ADJ N*

c) She came from a poor family, but eventually she became **rich**. *ADJ N*

d) Some people believe that the **rich** should contribute more to charities. *ADJ N*

e) We worry about **homeless** people when the weather turns cold. *ADJ N*

f) The mayor wants to build a new shelter for the **homeless**. *ADJ N*

g) The woman was overjoyed by the **news** that her brother would soon visit.

h) Television **news** stations report on world events, local events, and the weather.

4. **Underline** all the **nouns** used as **adjectives**. **Circle** all the **adjectives** used as **nouns**.

a) The young plumber soon fixed the clogged bathtub drain.

b) The young and the elderly suffer most from the flu that is going around.

c) We bring the patio furniture indoors before the first winter storm.

d) Only the wealthy can afford these expensive sports cars.

e) The hopeful find joy in the world to make themselves and others happy.

f) I bought a package of colourful gel pens and a pink note pad.

g) Only the tough are brave enough to try the hot peppers.

h) Of all the tarts my mother made, the strawberry is my favourite.

i) My night table holds my book, my lamp, and my alarm clock.

5. Circle **ADJ** if the bold word is used as an **adjective**. Circle **ADV** if the bold word is used as an **adverb**.

   a) Try to come **early** if you want to get a good seat for the concert. **ADJ ADV**

   b) The **early** election results suggest that it will be a close election. **ADJ ADV**

   c) I might arrive **late** for the meeting if the traffic is bad. **ADJ ADV**

   d) Luke was tired because he had stayed up to watch a **late** movie. **ADJ ADV**

   e) The outfielder jumped **high** to catch the baseball as it sailed overhead. **ADJ ADV**

   f) The lawyer tried **hard** to convince the jury that the woman was innocent. **ADJ ADV**

   g) My grandmother adopted the **sweetest** kitten I've ever seen. **ADJ ADV**

   h) Even the **bravest** knight was nervous as he walked up to the dragon. **ADJ ADV**

6. What is the **bold adverb** describing? Circle **V** for a verb, **ADJ** for an adjective, or **ADV** for an adverb.

   a) It is **extremely** unlikely that the stolen jewels will ever be found. **V ADJ ADV**

   b) Jane **often** forgets to set her alarm clock before she goes to sleep. **V ADJ ADV**

   c) The stray dog ate **so** quickly that I knew it must be starving. **V ADJ ADV**

   d) I didn't want to wake her if she was asleep, so I knocked **quite** softly. **V ADJ ADV**

   e) He will have to try **harder** if he wants to improve his marks. **V ADJ ADV**

   f) The weather is **unusually** warm for April, don't you think? **V ADJ ADV**

   g) It is **extremely** dangerous to swim in the ocean when sharks are near.
     V ADJ ADV

   h) Jenn **always** skips into her room and jumps into bed at night. **V ADJ ADV**

Action Verbs and Linking Verbs

Most verbs identify the action that someone or something is doing. These verbs are called **action verbs**. Look at the examples below.

*Examples: Huge waves **crash** against the shore.*
*Walter often **writes** to grandfather in Arizona.*
*The hungry cat **pounced** on the mouse.*

Notice how the verb in each sentence below does **not** identify an action that someone or something did or is doing.

*Examples: The sky **was** grey.*
*Bob **seems** happy with his new computer.*
*Tracey **is** my cousin.*

In these sentences, the sky, Bob, and Tracey aren't actively doing anything. Verbs that do not show action are called **linking verbs**.

A linking verb links the subject with information provided in the predicate.

Subject + Linking Verb + An adjective that describes the subject
OR
A noun that is another name for the subject

Let's look again at the sentences with examples of linking verbs.

Example: The sky was grey.
The subject is *sky*. The linking verb *was* connects the subject with the adjective *grey*, which is in the predicate. *Grey* describes the noun *sky*.

Example: Bob seems happy with his new computer.
The subject is *Bob*. The linking verb *seems* connects the subject with the adjective *happy,* which is in the predicate. *Happy* describes *Bob*.

Example: Tracey is my cousin.
The subject is *Tracey*. The linking verb *is* connects the subject with the noun *cousin,* which is in the predicate. *Cousin* is another name for *Tracey*. (You could call Tracey *my cousin* instead of using her name.)

All forms (past, present, and future) of the verbs *to be* (*am, is, are, was, were, be, been, being*) and *to seem* (*seem, seems, seemed*) are linking verbs.

Linking verbs are often used with helping verbs. Look at the examples below.

*Examples: The movie **should be** interesting. I **might be** too busy to watch it.*

Action Verbs and Linking Verbs (continued)

1. The **linking verb** in each sentence is in bold. Underline the **simple subject**. In the predicate, circle the **adjective** that describes the subject **or** the **noun** that is another name for the subject. Then **circle** the correct answer in the next sentence.

   a) The baby **is** very cute.
      The linking verb connects the subject to (an adjective   a noun).

   b) Mr. Kapoor **is** the principal of our school.
      The linking verb connects the subject to (an adjective   a noun).

   c) These recipes **are** very complicated.
      The linking verb connects the subject to (an adjective   a noun).

   d) Those people **were** quite rude to me.
      The linking verb connects the subject to (an adjective   a noun).

   e) Mrs. Robertson **was** my teacher last year.
      The linking verb connects the subject to (an adjective   a noun).

   f) An accident up ahead **is** the reason for this traffic jam.
      The linking verb connects the subject to (an adjective   a noun).

2. Underline the **linking verb** and any **helping verbs**. In the predicate, circle the **adjective** that describes the subject **or** the **noun** that is another name for the subject.

   a) This character might be the hero in the story.

   b) The introduction in my speech should be shorter.

   c) My brother did seem a bit irritated yesterday.

   d) The children are being quiet during this long journey.

   e) This fingerprint could be an important clue.

   f) My friends might seem silly at first.

   g) She will be a famous athlete someday.

   h) Having the party on the weekend would be better.

   i) Jennie and Erik have been gone a long time.

More Linking Verbs

The verbs *to be* and *to seem* are two common linking verbs. Below are a few examples of other verbs that can be linking verbs.

to appear   to become   to feel   to look   to smell   to sound   to taste

Some words can be used as an action verb or a linking verb.

Linking verb: *The soup **smelled** good.*

Soup does not have a nose to smell with, so the soup is not doing the action of smelling something. In this sentence, *smelled* is a linking verb. The verb is linking the subject (*soup*) with an adjective that describes the subject (*good*).

Action verb: *The children **smelled** smoke.*

In this sentence, the children are doing the action of smelling, so *smelled* is an action verb.

One way to tell whether a verb is a linking verb or an action verb is to replace the verb with *am, is,* or *are* and see whether the sentence still makes sense. If it does, the verb is probably a linking verb.

*Example: The soup ~~smelled~~ **is** good.*

The meaning of the original sentence has changed a little, but the new sentence still makes sense. The verb *smelled* is a linking verb in this sentence.

*Example: The children ~~smelled~~ **are** smoke.*

The new sentence does not make sense. The verb *smelled* is an action verb in this sentence.

NOTE: The test of replacing the verb with *am, is,* or *are* does **not** work with some verbs, such as *to appear* and *to look*.

Action verb: *A mouse **appeared** in the doorway.*
         *A mouse ~~appeared~~ **is** in the doorway.*

The sentence still makes sense when you replace the verb *appeared* with *is,* but *appeared* is an action verb in the sentence.

To be certain, check to see if the verb links the subject to an adjective that describes the subject, or to a noun that is another name for the subject. If the verb does one of these things, it is a linking verb.

More Linking Verbs (continued)

1. Underline the verb. Circle **AV** if the verb is an action verb, or **LV** if the verb is a linking verb.

   a) The gardener grew several kinds of tulips. **AV LV**

   b) Sally grew quite tall. **AV LV**

   c) The traveller felt lonely during the long trip. **AV LV**

   d) Juan felt the bump on the back of his head. **AV LV**

   e) We turned our guest bedroom into an exercise room. **AV LV**

   f) Billy's face turned red with embarrassment. **AV LV**

   g) The women had been smelling a variety of perfumes at the store. **AV LV**

   h) The man appeared tired after the long hike. **AV LV**

   i) We could keep these postcards as souvenirs of our vacation. **AV LV**

2. Underline the complete verb (including any helping verbs). Circle **AV** if the verb is an action verb, or **LV** if the verb is a linking verb.

   a) Rhonda and I might become friends. **AV LV**

   b) Winston has been awake all night. **AV LV**

   c) A security guard will sound the alarm. **AV LV**

   d) The scientists had proven their theory. **AV LV**

   e) We must stay calm in the face of danger. **AV LV**

   f) All passengers should remain in their seats during takeoff. **AV LV**

   g) A rainbow might appear after the downpour. **AV LV**

   h) I looked everywhere for the key to my bicycle lock. **AV LV**

   i) The old wooden staircase looked unsafe. **AV LV**

   j) The spectators went crazy after the winning goal. **AV LV**

Direct Objects of Verbs

A **direct object** is the person or thing (noun or pronoun) that receives the action named by an action verb. To find the direct object in a sentence, follow these steps:

1. Identify the simple subject of the sentence.

*Example: The noisy **children** chased the dog around the yard.*

The simple subject is *children*.

2. Identify the action verb that tells what the subject is doing.

*Example: The noisy **children** <u>chased</u> the dog around the yard.*

The action verb is *chased*.

3. Create a question as shown below.

Simple subject + action verb + *whom or what*?

For the example sentence above, you would create this question:

Children <u>chased</u> *whom or what?* (Answer: *the dog*)

The answer to the question is the direct object. In the example sentence, *the dog* is the direct object of the action verb *chased*.

Sometimes an action verb has more than one direct object. Look at the example below.

*Example: **Lars** often <u>helps</u> Eddie and Nancy.*

Lars <u>helps</u> *whom or what?* (Answer: *Eddie and Nancy*)

In the example sentence, *Eddie and Nancy* are the direct objects of the action verb *helps*.

An action verb doesn't always have a direct object.

*Example: The **musicians** <u>played</u> beautifully last night.*

Musicians <u>played</u> *whom or what?*

The sentence does not provide an answer to the question, so the action verb *played* has no direct object.

*Example: The **musicians** <u>played</u> the song beautifully last night.*

Musicians <u>played</u> *whom or what?* (Answer: *the song*)

In this version of the sentence, *the song* is the direct object of the action verb *played*.

Direct Objects of Verbs (continued)

1. **Underline** the action verb and **circle** the direct object or objects.

   a) The teacher collected the quizzes from the students.

   b) An archeologist discovered ancient fossils near the lake.

   c) Anna and Michelle ate lunch on the patio.

   d) A tornado damaged the library and the hospital.

   e) According to news reports, someone deliberately set the fire.

   f) The basketball team won the championship game and a trophy.

   g) The doctor prescribed medicine for my sore throat.

   h) Snow covered the streets, sidewalks, and cars.

   i) Sofia and her sister watched *The Wizard of Oz* on TV.

Remember that an action verb does not always have a direct object. A linking verb is not an action verb, so a linking verb does not have a direct object.

2. **Underline** the verb. **Circle** any direct objects in the sentence.

   a) My friends and I painted the garage last summer.

   b) Dad put a sandwich, yogurt, and an apple in my lunch bag.

   c) People often feel sleepy after a large meal.

   d) Scientists carefully examined the fossil.

   e) The children played happily in the sandbox.

   f) A stranger rescued a man and a child from the burning house.

   g) Ahmad wrote a story about his pet cat.

   h) The weather was sunny and warm all week long.

   i) The students seemed relieved after the test.

Canadian Grammar Practice 6 © Chalkboard Publishing

Indirect Objects of Verbs

A **direct object** is the person or thing (noun or pronoun) that receives the action named by an action verb. The direct object answers the question "Whom or what?" after the verb.

Example: Marco bought a gift.

Marco bought whom or what? (Answer: *a gift*)

In the example sentence, *a gift* is the direct object of the action verb *bought*.

An **indirect object** is the person or thing (noun or pronoun) that receives the direct object, or the person or thing the direct object is for.

*Example: Marco bought **his brother** a gift.*

In this sentence, *his brother* is the **indirect object** of the action verb *bought*. The direct object (*a gift*) is *for* his brother.

To find the indirect object in a sentence, create two questions as shown below.

Action verb + direct object + *to whom or what?*

Action verb + direct object + *for whom or what?*

For the example sentence above, you would create these questions:

Bought a gift to whom or what? (The sentence does not provide an answer to this question.)

Bought a gift for whom or what? (Answer: *his brother*)

You will be able to answer one of the questions. The answer is the **indirect object**. For the example sentence, the indirect object of the action verb *bought* is *his brother*.

Below is another example.

Example: The artist showed me her lovely paintings.

The **direct object** of the action verb *showed* is *paintings*.

Showed paintings to whom or what? (Answer: *me*)

Showed paintings for whom or what? (The sentence does not provide an answer.)

The **indirect object** of the action verb *showed* is *me*.

Remember:
• Only a sentence with a direct object can have an indirect object.
• Some sentences have a direct object but no indirect object.
• Only action verbs can have direct objects and indirect objects.
• Linking verbs do not have direct objects or indirect objects.

Indirect Objects of Verbs (continued)

1. **Underline** each direct object and **circle** each indirect object.

   a) The storyteller tells the children stories.

   b) Ernesto gave the cashier his coupons.

   c) The children sang their parents a song.

   d) Mrs. Appleton bought her husband a gift.

   e) The dressmaker sewed Connie a dress.

   f) We sent Hans several photos.

   g) Dad bought my sister new shoes.

2. **Underline** each direct object. If there is an indirect object, **circle** it.

   a) A volunteer made us costumes for the play.

   b) My teammate threw me the ball.

   c) Gary received the letter yesterday morning.

   d) The gardener plants flowers every spring.

   e) The cashier handed Yu her change.

   f) Mom poured the sour milk down the drain.

   g) Ricardo got us tickets to the concert.

   h) The squirrel buried nuts by the oak tree.

   i) The spy passed his partner a note.

   j) The coach gave her team some suggestions.

   k) The chef roasted vegetables in the oven.

   l) The children made their father breakfast.

Verbs Review Quiz

1. Circle **AV** if the sentence contains an action verb. Circle **LV** if the sentence contains a linking verb.

   a) Many drivers in the traffic jam honked their horns. **AV LV**

   b) The boy in the blue coat seems upset about something. **AV LV**

   c) The children are being cooperative today. **AV LV**

   d) Two babies on the bus cried loudly. **AV LV**

   e) The squirrels quickly buried acorns for the winter. **AV LV**

   f) The weather was very cold and snowy this week. **AV LV**

   g) Kelly rode her new bike to the library and back. **AV LV**

   h) My birthday will be on Tuesday this year. **AV LV**

2. The sentences below contain linking verbs. **Circle** the simple subject. Draw a **single underline** below an adjective that describes the subject. Draw a **double underline** below a noun that is another name for the subject.

   a) Karen will be the leader of the group.

   b) The consequences of his foolish actions have been serious.

   c) Mr. Walker had been an engineer for many years.

   d) Our hard work will seem worthwhile in the future.

   e) This science project will take a long time to finish.

   f) My friend Tao is fluent in three languages.

   g) Spring has been my favourite season so far this year.

   h) My busy mother appears to be deep in thought.

Verbs Review Quiz (continued)

3. **Underline** any **linking verbs** (including helping verbs). Remember that some verbs can be used as an action verb or a linking verb.

a) Maria has tasted the steaming chicken soup.

b) The soup did taste a bit too salty.

c) I felt hungry after my long walk.

d) Roger appeared quite relaxed before his speech to the class.

e) The excited child will become calm after a while.

f) I felt a caterpillar crawling up my leg.

g) After your fall, a bruise might appear on your leg.

h) These shoes look much too small for me.

i) Our trip to the beach could be the best trip of the summer.

j) Sandy appeared to be sick this morning.

k) Carlos was riding his bike in the park yesterday.

l) The pizza must be ready by now.

m) The doctor's office smells of alcohol.

n) We saw a deer in the woods when we went hiking.

o) A camping trip sounds good!

p) That tiny sprout will become a huge sunflower plant.

Canadian Grammar Practice 6 © Chalkboard Publishing

4. **Circle** only the action verbs. **Underline** any direct objects.

   a) We packed the delicate china and the crystal glasses very carefully.

   b) She put the wet clothes in the dryer.

   c) This new detergent removes almost any stain.

   d) Owen felt ill after the roller coaster ride.

   e) The hockey player raced down the ice.

   f) He seemed distracted during the debate.

   g) Mrs. Gomez cut the grass and watered the garden.

   h) Hold your breath, and then dive into the water.

   i) Lionel washed his hands and face before dinner.

5. **Underline** each direct object. If there is an indirect object, **circle** it.

   a) Please tell me your ideas.

   b) We bought the dog a new collar yesterday.

   c) Ali found his hat in his coat pocket.

   d) The carpenter built us a new bookshelf.

   e) Give Mrs. St. Pierre my best wishes.

   f) We sent the mayor an invitation to the big event.

   g) The voice on the phone sounded unfamiliar.

   h) He put the blue suitcase back in the closet.

   i) Uncle Jonas sent me tickets for the baseball game.

   j) I lent my friend two comic books and a novel.

Punctuating Dialogue

Use **quotation marks** around words that someone is speaking.

Examples: "Don't forget to take your umbrella," <u>said Dad</u>.
"The experiment produced interesting results," <u>the scientist explained.</u>
"Let's give Mom her gift after breakfast," <u>whispered Demi.</u>

The underlined words are called **speaker tags**. A speaker tag tells who is talking.

When the speaker tag comes **after** the spoken words, remember to put a comma **before** the **second** quotation mark. (See the examples above.)
BUT …

Do not put a comma before the second quotation mark if there is a question mark or exclamation point at the end of the spoken words.

Examples: "How could I have forgotten Ted's birthday?" Gary asked himself.
"Watch out for that car!" exclaimed Valerie.

If the speaker tag comes **before** the spoken words, put a comma **after** the speaker tag.

Example: My cousin said, "You should come to visit us next summer."
Remember to use a **capital letter** for the first spoken word.

---

1. Add **quotation marks** to each sentence below. Add a **comma** if necessary.

   a) Could you tell me if there is a gas station nearby?   the driver asked.

   b) The salesperson said   This shirt is also available in blue and green.

   c) Get off of my lawn!   the woman shouted angrily at the children.

   d) Please speak louder so everyone can hear   the teacher requested.

   e) The plumber said   I have replaced the leaky pipe in the basement.

   f) I have so much homework to do tonight   groaned Paul.

   g) Who was making all that noise?   Mom asked us.

   h) The experts said that finding a solution would take time   reported the mayor.

   i) We won the game! We won!   the players cheered loudly.

Canadian Grammar Practice 6 © Chalkboard Publishing

Punctuating Dialogue (continued)

In your writing, if someone says a long sentence, you can often put the speaker tag in the middle of the sentence. Look at the example below.

Example: "I was on my way to work," said Mom, "when I realized that I had forgotten my lunch."

If you are putting the speaker tag in the middle of a spoken sentence, remember to do the following:

- Put **quotation marks** around the first part of the spoken sentence and the second part of the spoken sentence.
- Put a **comma** at the end of the first part of the spoken sentence, before the second quotation mark.
- Put a **comma** after the speaker tag.
- Put a **period**, **question mark**, or **exclamation point** at the end of the second part of the spoken sentence, before the last quotation mark.
- Remember that you **do not** need a **capital letter** on the first word of the **second part** of the spoken sentence, unless the word is *I* or a proper noun.

2. Add the **correct punctuation** to each sentence.

a) When I was your age   said Grandma   people used typewriters because nobody had computers at home

b) If you want to become successful   the speaker explained   you must work hard and not give up when you become discouraged

c) The coach told the players   I am so proud of your teamwork in tonight's game

d) Someone once stole this painting   said the museum guide   but the police caught the thief before he could sell it

e) You must be kidding   Sandra exclaimed in amazement when I told her what had happened

f) How could anyone do such a terrible thing   the man asked his wife.

g) If you are not sure how to punctuate this sentence   said the teacher   look back at the examples.

Try writing your own sentences with dialogue. Write sentences that have the speaker tag at the beginning, in the middle, and at the end of the sentence.

Using Commas

When you are writing, watch out for places where you need to use commas.

Commas in Lists

If a list has more than two items, use a comma after each item except the last item.

Example: Jupiter, Saturn, and Uranus are the largest planets in our solar system.

Each item in a list can be more than one word. Use a comma after each item except the last item.

Example: Riding a bike, walking to school, and playing sports are all good exercise.

Commas with *Yes* and *No*

Use a comma after *yes* or *no* when it appears at the beginning of a sentence.

Example: Yes, I do think Lu would be an excellent captain for our hockey team.

Commas with Questions

If you add a question at the end of a sentence, use a comma before the question.

Example: The weather is warm for April, isn't it?

Commas with Names

When someone is speaking and says the name of the person he or she speaking to, use a comma before and after the name.

Example: "By the way, Julian, I thought the speech you gave was excellent," I said.

If the name is at the beginning or end of the spoken words, use one comma to separate the name from the rest of the sentence.

*Examples: "Angela, could you please help me fold the laundry?" Mom asked.
The children said, "You made a great dinner tonight, Dad."*

Using Commas (continued)

Commas with Cities and Provinces

Use a comma between the name of a city and its province.

Example: Abdul has several friends who live in Calgary, Alberta.

If the name of the province is not at the end of the sentence, also use a comma after the name of the province.

Example: The Art Gallery of Ontario in Toronto, Ontario, has some wonderful paintings.

Using Commas with Dialogue

See "Punctuating Dialogue" on pages 68–69 for information on using commas with dialogue.

1. Add **commas** where necessary to the sentences below.

   a) I think Amelia plays soccer doesn't she?

   b) Rodrigo had a nap after washing the dishes drying them and putting them away.

   c) Dinosaur Provincial Park in Drumheller Alberta is a popular tourist attraction.

   d) "Lauren do you need a ride to baseball practice?" I asked.

   e) We could use glue nails or screws to fasten together the two boards.

   f) No I can't go to the movies on Thursday evening because I have choir practice.

   g) "John you like pasta don't you?" Mrs. Greenburg asked.

   h) My grandparents recently moved to Gander Newfoundland.

   i) "Yes I'll call you tomorrow Uncle Ken" Sam said.

   j) We visited a seafood festival the public gardens and historic sites in Halifax Nova Scotia.

   k) The fossils in the Royal BC Museum in Victoria British Columbia are amazing.

2. Check the sentences below for correct use of **commas**. If you find a comma that is not necessary, cross it out. Add any commas that are missing.

   a) "Lukas, asks interesting questions doesn't he?" the teacher remarked.

   b) Regina, and Saskatoon, are two of the largest cities in Saskatchewan.

   c) "Lindsay, you're going to come with us aren't you?" Mom asked.

   d) In Banff, Alberta the famous Lake Louise and Banff National Park, are popular tourist attractions.

   e) "No I am not allergic, to eggs, peanuts or lobster," I explained.

   f) Susie, picked up her hat, mittens and coat, but forgot her scarf.

   g) The apple, blossoms were, swarming with bees flies and other flying insects.

   h) "Do you, want to eat dinner with us Jeff?" Katy, asked.

3. Add **quotations** and **other punctuation** wherever necessary.

   a) When I was a little girl said Grandma we walked a mile to school every day

   b) I want to go with you shouted the girl

   c) Tabby's kittens were named Fluffy Bitsy Mittens and Socks

   d) Ken cut up apples bananas oranges and grapes for his fruit salad

   e) I am going to make a fun cake for your birthday Aunt May said to Mike

   f) Watch out the boy warned as he sped past me on his bike

   g) Alice are you sure you multiplied those numbers correctly Dad asked

   h) Nothing could make me unhappy today said Tony with a smile

Using Colons and Semicolons

Using Colons

1. Use a colon before giving a list of three or more people or things.

Example: I have three favourite fruits: apples, oranges, and grapes.

The words before the colon should communicate a complete thought. **Do not** use a colon after a linking verb.

Examples:
Incorrect: *The best players on my team are: Yolanda, Anna, and Penny.*
Correct: *The best players on my team are Yolanda, Anna, and Penny.*
Correct: *There are three great players on my team: Yolanda, Anna, and Penny.*

2. Use a colon between the hour and minutes when giving a time.

Example: I have a dentist appointment at 10:15 tomorrow morning.

3. Use a colon between the title and subtitle of a book.

Example: Mr. Chu wrote a book called Free to Fly: Conquering Your Fear of Flying.

Using Semicolons

1. Use a semicolon to join two sentences whose meanings are closely related.

Two sentences: *Rain was pouring down. Tim's clothes got very wet.*
Joined with semicolon: *Rain was pouring down; Tim's clothes got very wet.*

The two short sentences above can be joined with a semicolon because their meanings are closely related. Tim's clothes got wet because it was raining.

Example: Julie went fishing on Saturday; her sister stayed home to study.

A semicolon is correct in this example because both parts of the sentence are closely related. Both parts tell what the girls did on Saturday.

The pairs of sentences below **cannot** be joined with semicolons. The sentences in each pair are not closely related in meaning.

Examples: The goldfish belong to my brother. He plays piano very well.

The dog chewed up my running shoes. We got her at an animal shelter.

The sun slowly set behind the mountains. I want to climb a mountain one day.

2. Use a semicolon between items in a list if one or more of the list items contains a comma.

Example: We visited Toronto, Canada; Paris, France; and London, England.

Using Colons and Semicolons (continued)

1. Write the correct punctuation (**colon** or **semicolon**) inside each pair of square brackets. Leave the brackets empty if no punctuation is needed.

   a) Henry told me that the movie starts at 7[   ]00 p.m.

   b) There were several items on my shopping list[   ] tomatoes, milk, bread, tea, and flour.

   c) The school fair was amazing[   ] I've never had so much fun!

   d) I'm reading a book called *Choosing a Career*[   ] *Tips for Young People.*

   e) In the drawer were a thick, bulky sweater[   ] a faded, ripped pair of jeans[   ] and two pairs of old socks.

   f) The items that came in today's mail were[   ] an advertising flyer, a telephone bill, and an invitation to a New Year's party.

   g) The store had three flavours of yogurt[   ] strawberry, blueberry, and raspberry.

   h) This recipe is very easy to make[   ] it takes less than ten minutes.

   i) After the snowstorm, the roads were[   ] wet, slippery, and dangerous.

2. Put a **check mark** after each sentence that uses a semicolon **correctly**. Put an **X** after each sentence that uses a semicolon **incorrectly**.

   a) Pam's feet were sore; she had spent the day hiking in the woods. _____
   Pam's feet were sore; she rushed home to watch her favourite TV show. _____

   b) Chess is a challenging game; I got a chess set for my birthday last year. _____
   Chess is a challenging game; it takes years to play it really well. _____

   c) The phone rang long after midnight; everyone in the house woke up. _____
   The phone rang long after midnight; I had to get up early in the morning. _____

   d) I am happy with my new printer; it prints pages very quickly. _____
   I am happy with my new printer; it uses less ink than the old one. _____

   e) Clifford often used his microwave; it heated food much faster than his oven. _____
   Clifford often used his microwave; sometimes he ate in a restaurant. _____

   f) It has been a dry summer; the sky looks like a thunderstorm is coming. _____
   I decide not to walk the dog; the sky looks like a thunderstorm is coming. _____

Canadian Grammar Practice 6 © Chalkboard Publishing

Punctuation Review Quiz

1. Rewrite the sentences below, adding **quotation marks** and **other punctuation** where necessary.

   a) Science is my favourite subject said Alison

   _____

   b) Ari whispered Be quiet so you don't wake the baby

   _____

   c) Do you need any help sir Carla asked

   _____

   d) I can't believe it's true my father exclaimed

   _____

2. Rewrite the sentences below. Move the **speaker tag** so that it is **not** at the beginning or end of the sentence. Adjust the **punctuation** where necessary.

   a) "Dad needs the car tonight, so I can't drive you to Ravi's house," Mom explained.

   _____

   _____

   b) Dawn grumbled, "It seems as though I always get blamed, even when it's not my fault."

   _____

   _____

   c) "Thank you for entering the talent show, and I wish you all luck," the judge told the contestants.

   _____

   _____

Punctuation Review Quiz (continued)

3. In the sentences below, add **commas** where necessary.

   a) "Gene you did a great job on this report!" said the teacher.

   b) My grandmother told me that she was born in Whitehorse Yukon.

   c) "Yes I did enjoy the movie" replied Fernando.

   d) "We've eaten at this restaurant before haven't we?" asked Aunt Selma.

   e) Milk cheese and yogurt are all good sources of calcium.

   f) "Asan you'll come to the park with us won't you?" she asked.

4. Rewrite each sentence, adding **colons**, **semicolons**, and **commas** where necessary.

   a) Yes I can come at 1015 tomorrow morning.

   _____

   b) We will visit three cities Ottawa Ontario Calgary Alberta and Iqaluit Nunavut.

   _____

   _____

   c) The book is called *I Laughed Out Loud Best Jokes for Kids.*

   _____

5. Put a **check mark** after each sentence that uses a semicolon **correctly**. Put an **X** after each sentence that uses a semicolon **incorrectly**.

   a) Our new house will not be ready on time; bad weather has delayed construction. ____
      Our new house will not be ready on time; I will finally have my own bedroom. ____

   b) This dryer dries clothes very quickly; it has been making strange noises lately. ____
      Something is wrong with the dryer; it has been making strange noises lately. ____

   c) I decided not to go jogging; my left knee has been a bit sore lately. ____
      I decided not to go jogging; I don't like jogging in this very cold weather. ____

What's the Correct Word?

Good or Well?

Good is an adjective, so use it to describe a noun or pronoun. *Well* is most often used as an adverb, and usually it describes a verb. Look at the sentence below.

Example: Arthur sang _____ during choir practice. (Use good or well?)

To choose the correct word, you need to decide whether the sentence needs an adjective or an adverb. In the example sentence above, the missing word will describe the verb *sang*, so the adverb *well* is the correct choice.

Examples: I am feeling good today.
I am feeling well today.

Both of the sentences above are correct. Why? In both sentences, the verb *feeling* is a linking verb. A linking verb can be followed by an adjective describing the noun that is the subject. So it is correct to say, "I am feeling good today." *Well* can be used as an adjective meaning "healthy," so it is also correct to say, "I am feeling well today."

Bad or Badly?

Bad is an adjective, so use it to describe a noun or pronoun. *Badly* is an adverb that is used to describe a verb.

Example: Nikki felt _____ after she yelled at her best friend. (Use bad or badly?)

In the sentence above, *felt* is a linking verb, so it is correct to use the adjective *bad* to describe the noun *Nikki*. You would not use the adverb *badly* to describe the noun *Nikki*.

Example: Hai played _____ in last night's hockey game. (Use bad or badly?)

In the sentence above, the missing word will describe the action verb *played*, **not** the noun *Hai*. An adverb is needed, so *badly* is the correct choice.

Real or Really?

Real is an adjective, so use it to describe a noun. *Really* is an adverb that is often used to describe an adjective, but it can also describe another adverb.

Example: We often eat at this restaurant because the food is _____ good.
    (Use real or really?)

The missing word needs to describe the adjective *good*, so the adverb *really* is correct.

Example: A jeweller said the necklace has _____ diamonds, not fake ones.
    (Use real or really?)

The missing word needs to describe the noun *diamonds*, so the adjective *real* is the correct choice.

What's the Correct Word? (continued)

Circle the correct word in brackets. Then complete the next sentence to explain your choice.

Example: The furnace has been working (good (well)) since we got it fixed.
I chose an (adjective (adverb)) that describes the (noun (verb)) working.

a) Alfonso studied more, and now he feels (good well) about his chances of passing.

I chose an (adjective adverb) that describes the (pronoun verb)

_____.

b) I am sure that we'll have a (real really) fun time at the amusement park.

I chose an (adjective adverb) that describes the (adjective noun verb)

_____.

c) They built the tree house (bad badly), and the next strong windstorm knocked it down.

I chose an (adjective adverb) that describes the (noun verb)

_____.

d) The doctor told his patient that she was not (good well) enough to return to work yet.

I chose an (adjective adverb) that describes the (pronoun verb)

_____.

e) When you eat (good well), your body gets the nutrition it needs.

I chose an (adjective adverb) that describes the (pronoun verb)

_____.

f) The children felt (bad badly) about forgetting their father's birthday.

   I chose an (adjective adverb) that describes the (noun verb)

   _____.

g) In the attic, we discovered a trunk filled with (real really) old clothes.

   I chose an (adjective adverb) that describes the (adjective noun verb)

   _____.

h) I wore the red sweater because red looks (good well) on me.

   I chose an (adjective adverb) that describes the (noun verb)

   _____.

i) The artist painted a (real really) beautiful portrait of my mother.

   I chose an (adjective adverb) that describes the (adjective noun verb)

   _____.

j) The milk smelled (bad badly), so I didn't drink it.

   I chose an (adjective adverb) that describes the (noun verb)

   _____.

k) We had our picnic basket packed, and the weather forecast looked (good well).

   I chose an (adjective adverb) that describes the (noun verb)

   _____.

l) I feel (bad badly) that you didn't get a piece of the cake.

   I chose an (adjective adverb) that describes the (pronoun verb)

   _____.

Write the Correct Word

Don't be confused by the words below. Always check your writing to make sure you have written the correct words.

Word	Definition and Example
accept	to receive or agree to something; to take something offered *Example: If the company offers me a great job, I will **accept** it.*
except	not including *Example: We will be busy every day this week, **except** Thursday.*
effect	a change or result that is caused by something else *Example: One **effect** of the snowstorm was that schools were closed.*
affect	to cause a change in someone or something *Example: His broken leg will **affect** his plans to go skiing next week.*
advice	a suggestion of what someone should do *Example: The teacher gave me **advice** on how to improve my writing.*
advise	to give a suggestion about what someone should do *Example: I **advise** you to study more if you want to improve your marks.*

1. **Circle** the correct word in brackets.

a) It is good to ask for (advice advise) when you have a difficult problem.

b) People often give a brief speech when they (accept except) an award.

c) Flooding was one (effect affect) of the heavy rainfall.

d) The hardware store is open every day (accept except) holidays.

e) "I (advice advise) you to get more exercise," said the doctor.

f) Eating too much junk food may eventually (effect affect) your health.

g) The person selling the car did not (accept except) the price I offered.

h) Officials hope the lower speed limit will (effect affect) the number of car accidents.

i) Lowering the speed limit had an (effect affect) on the number of car accidents.

j) She is very wise, so you should pay attention to her (advice advise)

Write the Correct Word (continued)

Make sure you use the words below correctly in your writing.

Word	Definition and Example
weather	the conditions outside, such as air temperature and cloudiness *Example: We hope the **weather** is good during our camping trip.*
whether	a word used when giving choices or possibilities; often used with *or not* *Example: We couldn't decide **whether** to watch a movie or play video games.*
raise	to lift or move something to a higher position or level *Example: Please **raise** your hand if you want to ask a question.*
rise	to move upward or become higher *Example: The sun will **rise** at 6:20 tomorrow morning.*
beside	next to; at the side of *Example: Tanya sat **beside** me at the concert.*
besides	other than *Example: No one **besides** me knew the secret.*

2. **Circle** the correct word in brackets.

a) We watched the hot-air balloon (raise rise) up into the sky.

b) (Beside Besides) one fingerprint, the police had no clues to help solve the crime.

c) We are wondering (weather whether) to paint this room or put up wallpaper.

d) He was so sleepy this morning that he could hardly (raise rise) his head from the pillow.

e) It will be more convenient to put the printer (beside besides) the computer.

f) They often eat dinner on the patio when the (weather whether) is nice.

g) As construction continued, we watched the new office tower (raise rise).

h) The detective wondered (weather whether) or not the woman had told the truth.

i) If we (raise rise) the picture on the wall, we can put the bookshelf beneath it.

j) I didn't know anyone at the party (beside besides) the person who had invited me.

k) Our flight to Ottawa was cancelled because of the stormy (weather whether).

Double Negatives

A double negative is a sentence that contains two negative words.

What Are Negative Words?

Below are the most common negative words:

no   not   none   no one   nothing   nowhere   nobody   never

Contractions made from a verb + *not* are also negative words. Here are some examples:

doesn't   isn't   wasn't   wouldn't   couldn't   shouldn't   won't   can't   don't

Why Are Double Negatives a Problem?

Double negatives are a problem because they often mean the opposite of what you really want to say. Look at the examples below:

Example: **Incorrect:** *Tomas spent all his money. Now he **doesn't** have **no** money.*

In the second sentence above, notice that both bold words are negatives. The sentence is a double negative. Think carefully about what the second sentence means. If Tomas does **not** have **no** money, then he must have some money. To correct the sentence, rewrite it so that it contains just one of the negative words.

Examples: **Correct:** *Now he **doesn't** have any money.*
Correct: *Now he has **no** money.*

Below is another example of a double negative.

Example: **Incorrect:** *Mrs. Soto is always very busy. She **never** has **no** time to relax.*

The second sentence is a double negative. The sentence actually means that Mrs. Soto always has some time to relax. Correct the sentence by rewriting it so that it contains just one of the negative words.

Examples: **Correct:** *She **never** has any time to relax.*
Correct: *She has **no** time to relax.*

Make sure your sentences say what you really mean. Avoid double negatives when you are speaking or writing.

Double Negatives (continued)

1. The sentences below are all **incorrect** double negatives. **Underline** the negative words in each sentence. Then **rewrite** the sentence so that it contains just one negative word.

a) Don't say nothing about the surprise party!

_____

b) I couldn't find my watch nowhere.

_____

c) We won't never go to that restaurant again.

_____

d) You can't trust no one these days.

_____

e) That show is not on TV no more.

_____

f) You shouldn't tell no one our secret.

_____

2. Write **two** ways of correcting each double negative below.

a) My sister has freckles, but I don't have none.

_____

_____

b) There isn't no easy answer to that question.

_____

_____

Identifying Errors

1. Use the letter codes below to identify **errors** in the sentences. A sentence may have more than one error or no errors.

Letter Code	Error
A	The final punctuation mark is not correct for the sentence type.
B	One or more words need a capital letter.
C	The antecedent of a pronoun is unclear.
D	A pronoun and its antecedent do not agree in number or gender.
E	A comma is missing or used incorrectly.
F	The sentence contains a double negative.
G	A word has been used incorrectly because it sounds or looks like the correct word.
H	An adjective needs to be replaced by an adverb.

a) Rani told her sister that she is very good at math. _____

b) How could I make such a silly mistake! _____

c) We went to the greek restaurant but unfortunately it was closed. _____

d) If you can't hear someone, politely ask them to speak louder. _____

e) The doctor said "These pills might have the affect of making you sleepy." _____

f) I know I sang bad, but I hope no one noticed accept you. _____

g) If Mike or Danny can come early, they can help us get ready. _____

h) I tried to help her, but she didn't want no advise from me. _____

i) If the detective finds fingerprints or a hair, she can use it as evidence. _____

j) The second world war effected people in many countries. _____

Canadian Grammar Practice 6 © Chalkboard Publishing

Identifying Errors (continued)

k) Mom asked aunt Penny if she liked her new car. _____

l) The pirate never told nobody where he had buried his treasure. _____

m) Kylie is real confident that the whether will improve this afternoon. _____

n) I wonder if Amita, Theo, and Sara, will come to the party? _____

o) You can invite your friends for the weekend, and she can sleep on the couch. _____

2. Find and correct **26 errors** in these paragraphs. Read the paragraphs, then rewrite them correctly in your notebook. When you are finished, reread your paragraphs to make sure they make sense.

On sunday, Carrie went to her sister kate's house four lunch. Kate made spaghetti and sauce. Carrie told her sister that she liked spaghetti? Kate brought out everything accept the grated cheese. Carrie got the cheese and placed it besides Kate. Halfway through her lunch! Carrie remembered she had an assignment do on tuesday. Carrie felt badly that she had not done no work. She needed to choose a subject do some research and write a report. If her did not hand in a report, they would effect her mark. Carrie's sister adviced her to go straight home after lunch and work on her project,

What subject would she choose. Carrie did not know weather she wanted to write about lions or about hippos. She knew a lot about lions, but she didn't know nothing about hippos. Carrie chose hippos for a really challenge, She worked hard on her report and handed them in on Tuesday. The next week, Carrie ran to Kate's house to show them the well mark she got on her project. Carrie told Kate she was real happy she had taken her advise.

Correcting Errors: "Disaster Cake"

Find and correct **29 errors** in this story.

1 My sister and I decided to make dad a birthday cake. Our parents were out shopping, so the birthday cake would be a surprise for him when they got home.

2 Rachel found a cake mix in the cupboard. She checked the directions. "We just need to add three ingredients; water, vegetable oil and eggs," she said.

3 "How do we make the icing" I asked.

4 "I found a can of iceing we can use," she replied "We have everything we need, accept birthday candles."

5 "I saw a box of birthday candles in the drawer by the sink," I said.

6 We got started. I poured the cake mix into a large bowl and Lisa added the water and vegetable oil. We took turns adding three eggs. I hit the first egg to hard against the edge of the bowl. The shell broke into lots of tiny peaces, and most of them went into the cake mix. We tried to pick them out.

7 "Don't worry if they're still a few pieces of eggshell in there," said Rachel. "They'll get smashed up when we use the mixer to beat everything together."

8 I got out the mixer and turned it on high. Everything was blending together nicely. Rachel said something, but I couldn't here her because the mixer made a lot of noise. "What did you say," I asked as I lifted the mixer out of the bowl. I should of turned them off first. Batter went flying all over the kitchen.

9 "Don't mix it no more," Rachel said in a frustrated voice. "Let's get this cake in the oven. We can clean up the mess you make while the cake bakes."

I poured the batter into a cake pan, and then Rachel carried the pan to the oven. "We forgot to preheat the oven" she exclaimed. "We'll just bake the cake at a higher temperature so it bakes faster." She put the cake into the oven and set it to a high temperature.

Just as we finished cleaning the kitchen, I smell something burning. "The cake is burnt on top!" I said as I opened the oven door.

"No one will see once we put the icing on," Rachel said. "Mom and Dad will be home any minute. We don't have no time to let it cool. Let's put the icing on write now."

The hot cake melted the icing, so it kept running off the cake. I was trying to put some icing back on top when I heard a car coming into the driveway.

"They're home! Put the candles on!" I yelled. Lisa found the box in the drawer and pulled out the candles. They had been used before, and now they were just ugly, short stubs of candles. We stuck it on the cake anyway.

"Happy Birthday Dad!" we shout as Mom and Dad come into the kichen. We held up the cake for them to see. They were quiet for a moment as they looked at are creation. Most of the icing had run off the top, and they could see the cake was burnt. Some little pieces of eggshell showed where there was no icing. The used candles didn't make the cake look any better.

"I'm sure it tastes better then it looks" Dad said. "It's the thought that counts. Thank you for making a birthday cake I'll certainly never forget!"

We all burst out laughing at the worst birthday cake ever.

Vocabulary List 1

---

obstacle

(noun) something that makes it difficult to accomplish a goal; something that is in your way and makes it to difficult to move forward
*The building's security alarm was an **obstacle** the burglars were not prepared for.*

---

abundant

(adjective) present or available in large numbers or amounts
*The explorers did not starve because they had an **abundant** supply of food.*

---

boisterous

(adjective) noisy and lively, possibly in an unpleasant way
*The **boisterous** party in the apartment next door kept me awake most of the night.*

---

coax

(verb) to persuade a person or animal to do something by talking in a gentle and friendly way
*The puppy was scared, but I eventually **coaxed** her to take a treat from my hand.*

---

inevitable

(adjective) unavoidable or sure to happen
*When you are first learning to skate, it is **inevitable** that you will fall a few times.*

---

credible

(noun) able to be believed; convincing
*The lawyer found out the witness lied about their employer, so nothing they told the court was **credible**.*

---

prefer

(verb) to like something more than something else
*She liked playing baseball and volleyball, but she **preferred** playing soccer.*

Canadian Grammar Practice 6 © Chalkboard Publishing

Vocabulary List 1 (continued)

In each sentence, write the **correct word** from the vocabulary list. For **verbs**, remember to use the correct form (singular or plural) and tense (past, present, or future).

a) The woman _____ her frightened cat to come out from under the couch.

b) We did not have a peaceful meal at the restaurant because there were several

_____ children at the next table.

c) The old man was known for telling tall tales, so he didn't sound _____ when he said saw a wolf in his yard.

d) If Michel wants to be a doctor, the biggest _____ he will need to overcome is his tendency to faint when he sees blood.

e) Nobody could run as fast as Christina, so it was _____ that she would win the race.

f) Before people started hunting whales in large numbers, these huge creatures were

_____ in the world's oceans.

g) Lorenzo's mother asked if he wanted soup or a sandwich for lunch. Lorenzo said he

would _____ a sandwich.

h) Mary said she saw Tara take Sami's book, but since Mary doesn't like Tara, her story

wasn't _____ .

i) _____ rain caused floods in some areas of the city.

j) If you don't watch where you are going when walking along a busy sidewalk, it is

_____ that you will bump into someone.

k) The _____ puppies barked and chased each other around the room.

Write your own sentences using the vocabulary words. Each sentence should clearly show the meaning of a vocabulary word.

Vocabulary List 1: Review

credible   obstacle   abundant   boisterous   coax   inevitable   preferred

1. Write the **correct** vocabulary word beside each definition. You may need to use some words more than once.

   a) _____: noisy and lively, possibly in an unpleasant way

   b) _____: unavoidable or sure to happen

   c) _____: present or available in large numbers or amounts

   d) _____: able to be believed; convincing

   e) _____: to like something more than something else

   f) _____: something that makes it difficult to accomplish a goal

2. Write the **correct** vocabulary word in each sentence. For **verbs**, remember to use the correct form (singular or plural) and tense (past, present, or future).

   a) I tried to _____ my shy daughter to sing a song for our guests.

   b) Lydia was given a seat in the middle of the row, but she said she would

   _____ to sit at the end.

   c) As people cleared land to build houses, trees became less _____.

   d) When my little brother becomes too _____, I try to calm him down.

   e) If you eat lots of sweets and never brush your teeth, it is _____ that you will get cavities.

   f) The reporter proved that his sources were _____, so the paper published his big news story.

   g) The secret of her success was that she never got discouraged when she faced an

   _____.

Vocabulary List 2

turmoil

(noun) a state of confusion or disorder in which people are upset or act in a disorganized way
*The city was in **turmoil** after the tornado damaged several neighbourhoods and left people without electricity.*

vow

(verb) to make a promise
*At the start of the new school year, Ayesha **vowed** to complete her assignments on time.*

(noun) a promise
*The new police officers made a **vow** to protect the community.*

inventory

(noun) a complete list of things that are in a place, such a store, box, or building
*The storekeeper took **inventory** of the frozen foods to find out what he needed to order.*

ample

(adjective) enough or more than enough
*There was **ample** room in the yard to build a swimming pool.*

recuperate

(verb) to get better after an illness, injury, or stress
*It took a few months for the hockey player to **recuperate** from back surgery.*

mimic

(verb) to copy or imitate someone or something, usually for fun

*The children **mimicked** the movements and sounds of farm animals.*
(Note the spelling change when adding an ending to *mimic*.)

refuge

(noun) protection or safety from danger, or a place that provides people or animals with protection or safety; *to take refuge* means to go to a safe place
*People who lived close to the forest fire took **refuge** at the school.*

Vocabulary List 2 (continued)

In each sentence, write the **correct word** from the vocabulary list. For **verbs**, remember to use the correct form (singular or plural) and tense (past, present, or future).

a) The research team _____ to find a way to cure the deadly disease.

b) There was _____ food to feed everyone at the wedding.

c) Jack took _____ of his baseball card collection to find out which cards he still needed.

d) I get very annoyed when my little brother and sister _____ everything I say or do.

e) Deanna's grandfather takes care of abandoned and abused pets at an animal

_____.

f) During the earthquake, the entire city was in _____.

g) Mom has been under a lot of stress at work lately, so Dad suggested that she take

some time off to _____.

h) When couples get married, they often make a _____ to love and take care of each other.

i) In dance class, the students learned a new dance by _____ the movements of the teacher.

j) Although the teacher gave students _____ time to complete the assignment, some students did not finish it on time.

k) To escape the dangerously hot desert sun, the explorers took _____ inside their tents.

l) Mr. Johan had a box of old comic books, and he took _____ of them to find out how much each comic was worth.

m) Tina will be away from school until she _____ from her illness.

Write your own sentences using the vocabulary words. Each sentence should clearly show the meaning of a vocabulary word.

Vocabulary List 2: Review

turmoil   vow   inventory   ample   recuperate   mimic   refuge

1. Write the **correct** vocabulary word beside each definition.

   a) _____: a promise

   b) _____: a complete list of things that are in a place

   c) _____: to get better after an illness, injury, or stress

   d) _____: to copy or imitate someone or something, usually for fun

   e) _____: a state of confusion or disorder in which people are
   upset or act in a disorganized way

   f) _____: a place that provides people or animals with protection
   or safety

   g) _____: enough or more than enough

2. Write the **correct** vocabulary word in each sentence. For **verbs**, remember to use
   the correct form (singular or plural) and tense (past, present, or future).

   a) The mother told her children that it was not polite to _____ their
   neighbour's accent.

   b) In medieval times, knights had to _____ to fight for their lords and
   serve them loyally. .

   c) After the accident, Jason had to miss a few weeks of school to _____.

   d) The coach took _____ of the football equipment to find out what the
   team needed for the next season.

   e) Liu selected a large suitcase because he needed _____ space to
   pack his clothes and books for college.

   f) Angry protestors blocked traffic and created _____ outside the hotel
   where the politician was speaking.

   g) For the talent show, Chantal _____ the sounds of several animals.

   h) The bus shelter provided _____ from the snow and chilly wind.

Vocabulary List 3

anguish

(noun) great pain or grief
*The dancer cried out in **anguish** when he landed on his injured foot.*

eavesdrop

(verb) to listen secretly to other people talking
*The man behind you is **eavesdropping** on our conversation.*

exotic

(adjective) unusual or from another country
*My grandmother's greenhouse is filled with **exotic** plants.*

proficient

(adjective) skilled or good at something
*Few people can beat Maya at chess because she is so **proficient** at the game.*

expanse

(noun) a large, open space or area
*The astronaut was amazed as she looked at the **expanse** of outer space.*

consent

(verb) to agree to or to give permission
*The nurse **consented** to the family's request to see the patient after visiting hours.*

(noun) agreement or permission
*If you want to go on the class trip, you must get the **consent** of a parent or guardian.*

baffling

(adjective) confusing or puzzling
*The pile of shredded toilet paper in the bathroom was **baffling**, since they didn't own a cat.*

Vocabulary List 3 (continued)

In each sentence, write the **correct word** from the vocabulary list. For **verbs**, remember to use the correct form (singular or plural) and tense (past, present, or future).

a) A _____ singer should have no problem singing this song.

b) I found out about their secret plan by _____.

c) The politician had refused several requests for an interview, but finally he

_____ to a brief telephone interview.

d) There were many valuable items in the house, so they were _____ that the burglars had stolen nothing but a box of old shoes.

e) In the past, traders rode camels on the long journey across the _____ of the great Sahara Desert.

f) The pet store had many _____ animals that I had never seen before.

g) Priya found the magazine article _____ because it contained many scientific terms that she did not understand.

h) The farmer was filled with _____ as his entire crop died from a mysterious disease.

i) I know I shouldn't have been _____, but I wanted to hear the man explain why he was so upset.

j) Rita begged to go to the mall with her friends, but her parents refused to give their

_____.

k) From the sidewalk, the family watched in _____ as the fire spread throughout their house.

l) The carpenter we hired is _____ at building kitchen cabinets.

m) Let's go to a restaurant that serves _____ foods from around the world.

Write your own sentences using the vocabulary words. Each sentence should clearly show the meaning of a vocabulary word.

Vocabulary List 3: Review

anguish   eavesdrop   exotic   proficient   expanse   consent   baffling

1. Write the **correct** vocabulary word beside each definition.

   a) _____ : skilled or good at something

   b) _____ : a large, open space or area

   c) _____ : great pain or grief

   d) _____ : unusual or from another country

   e) _____ : agreement or permission

   f) _____ : confusing or puzzling

   g) _____ : to listen secretly to other people talking

2. Write the **correct** vocabulary word in each sentence. For **verbs**, remember to use the correct form (singular or plural) and tense (past, present, or future).

   a) Dad has _____ to our plan to make a skating rink in the backyard.

   b) Over the school year, the students worked hard and became _____ in speaking French.

   c) The _____ of the wildlife park allows elephants, giraffes, lions, and many other wild animals to roam freely.

   d) The restaurant where my family and friends went for my birthday dinner served

   many _____ foods from various countries in Africa.

   e) How the dog had climbed up on the roof was _____ to everyone.

   f) Doctors could not perform the surgery until the woman gave her _____.

   g) I was annoyed that my brother had _____ on my phone call.

   h) The families of the miners were filled with _____ when they learned of the terrible mining accident.

Vocabulary List 4

duplicate

(verb; pronounced doo-pli-kate) to make a copy that is just like the original; to repeat
*Rajesh used a scanner to **duplicate** his sister's drawing.*

(noun; pronounced doo-pli-kit) an exact copy
*Dad got a **duplicate** of the front door key to leave with a neighbour.*

hoax

(noun) a joke or trick that is meant to fool someone
*The newspaper report about a lion escaping from the zoo turned out to be a **hoax**.*

beneficial

(adjective) helpful or leading to good results
*A good education is **beneficial** when someone is looking for a new job.*

hardy

(adjective) healthy and strong; able to survive challenges or difficult conditions
*The shipwrecked sailors were **hardy**, so they were able to survive on the desert island until they were rescued.*

quench

(verb) to satisfy thirst; to put something out (usually a fire)
*Foam from the fire extinguisher **quenched** the flames.*

feud

(noun) a nasty disagreement that has lasted a long time
*The **feud** between the two men started when one accused the other of lying.*

(verb) to take part in a nasty disagreement
*The children were **feuding** over which program to watch on TV.*

apprehensive

(adjective) nervous; concerned that something bad or unpleasant may happen
*Suki studied hard, but she still felt **apprehensive** about the test.*

Vocabulary List 4 (continued)

In each sentence, write the **correct word** from the vocabulary list. For **verbs**, remember to use the correct form (singular or plural) and tense (past, present, or future).

a) Naomi was _____ about showing her parents her report card.

b) For years, Mrs. Gordon and Mr. Santiago _____ about whether her fence was on his property.

c) A farmer told reporters that he had found buried pirate treasure on his land, but it turned out to be a _____.

d) The travellers stopped by the stream to rest, cool down, and _____ their thirst.

e) Exercise is _____ to your health and can even help you think more clearly.

f) Shaun is swimming in the race, and he hopes to _____ his record-setting time from the same event last year.

g) It was an unusually cool and dry summer, but the _____ plant continued to grow and produce flowers.

h) The _____ between the two kingdoms lasted 100 years and led to many battles.

i) To show her skill, the artist painted a _____ of a famous painting in the museum.

j) Having a group leader is _____ because a leader can make sure that everyone does a fair share of the work.

k) Firefighters used helicopters to _____ the flames before the forest fire destroyed more trees.

l) On the day of the piano recital, Zack felt _____ because he knew he had not practiced enough.

Write your own sentences using the vocabulary words. Each sentence should clearly show the meaning of a vocabulary word.

98   Canadian Grammar Practice 6 © Chalkboard Publishing

Vocabulary List 4: Review

duplicate   hoax   beneficial   hardy   quench   feud   apprehensive

1. Write the **correct** vocabulary word beside each definition.

   a) _____: a joke or trick that is meant to fool someone

   b) _____: an exact copy

   c) _____: able to survive challenges or difficult conditions

   d) _____: to take part in a nasty disagreement

   e) _____: nervous; concerned that something bad may happen

   f) _____: helpful or leading to good results

   g) _____: to put something out, such as a fire

2. Write the **correct** vocabulary word in each sentence. For **verbs**, remember to use the correct form (singular or plural) and tense (past, present, or future).

   a) The dressmaker tried to _____ a beautiful dress in a fashion magazine.

   b) The inventors finally asked a judge to settle their _____ over who had been first to invent the new kind of light bulb.

   c) A man said he'd seen a huge monster swimming in the lake, but most people

   believe the story is just a _____.

   d) The first settlers were _____ people who worked long hours to clear trees from the land and build log cabins by hand.

   e) It is _____ to show photos and diagrams during your presentation so people can see what you are describing.

   f) I made a _____ of the handout for my classmate who was absent today.

   g) The doctor's friendly face made Danielle feel less _____ about the surgery.

Vocabulary List 5

liberate

(verb) to free someone or something
*The women formed an organization to **liberate** children who were being used as slave workers.*

pedestrian

(noun) a person who is walking along a city road or street
*It is dangerous when a **pedestrian** is careless and forgets to pay attention to traffic when crossing the street.*

indispensable

(adjective) necessary; extremely important
*For many people, smartphones have become an **indispensable** tool that connects them with their friends and family.*

accumulate

(verb) to gather bit by bit; to increase in amount or number over time
*After the storm, snowplows removed the snow that had **accumulated** on city streets.*

corridor

(noun) a passageway or hallway in a building
*I heard echoes of my footsteps as I walked down the long **corridor** of the empty school.*

obvious

(adjective) easy to see, recognize, or understand
*The spy wore grey clothing so he would not be **obvious** in the crowd.*

ignite

(verb) to set on fire; to catch fire
*Some experts believe that the fire started when sparks flew from the machine and **ignited** dry leaves on the ground.*

Vocabulary List 5 (continued)

In each sentence, write the **correct word** from the vocabulary list. For **verbs**, remember to use the correct form (singular or plural) and tense (past, present, or future).

a) The cane was _____ to the elderly man because he could not walk very far without it.

b) The firefighters believe that it was a candle that _____ the curtains.

c) The driver quickly came to a stop when he saw the _____ in the middle of the road.

d) Maria held the book so tightly, it was _____ that she wanted to buy it.

e) At the school assembly, our principal reminded us not to loiter or play in the

_____ .

f) After months of caring for the injured bear cub, Fatima decided to _____ the animal by putting it back in the wild.

g) Jiang is very proud of her stamp and coin collection, which she _____ over many years.

h) Mom told me not to ride my skateboard on the sidewalk because I might crash

into a _____ .

i) I use the dictionary every day to help me when I'm reading and writing, so it is

_____ to me.

j) The guard opened the gate and _____ the prisoner from jail.

k) We have _____ so many items since moving into our house that there is not enough room to store them all.

l) At the hospital, two nurses quickly wheeled a patient down a _____ that led to the operating room

Write your own sentences using the vocabulary words. Each sentence should clearly show the meaning of a vocabulary word.

Vocabulary List 5: Review

liberate   pedestrian   indispensable   accumulate   corridor   obvious   ignite

1. Write the **correct** vocabulary word beside each definition.

   a) _____ : easy to see, recognize, or understand

   b) _____ : to catch fire

   c) _____ : extremely important

   d) _____ : to free someone or something

   e) _____ : to gather bit by bit

   f) _____ : a person who is walking along a city road or street

   g) _____ : a passageway or hallway in a building

2. Write the **correct** vocabulary word in each sentence. For **verbs**, remember to use the correct form (singular or plural) and tense (past, present, or future).

   a) The family organized a book sale to get rid of some of the books that they had

      _____ over the years.

   b) She turned red, making it _____ she was embarrassed.

   c) The building manager was upset because someone had sprayed graffiti all over

      the walls of the _____ .

   d) Someone had decided to open the cages at the zoo and _____
      the animals.

   e) Heat and hot water are _____ to everyone in Yukon during the
      winter.

   f) A _____ should wait patiently for the traffic light to turn green
      before crossing the street.

   g) Mom used a match to _____ the small pile of twigs that she
      had gathered to make a campfire.

Grammar Review Test

1. Add the correct **punctuation** at the end of the sentence. Write whether the sentence is **declarative**, **imperative**, **exclamatory**, or **interrogative**.

   a) That's a gigantic bunch of balloons   Sentence type: _____

   b) Please put your books away   Sentence type: _____

   c) Did you see that   Sentence type: _____

   d) I forgot to buy milk this week   Sentence type: _____

2. Circle the **complete subject** and underline the **complete predicate**.

   a) The quick brown fox jumped over the lazy dog.

   b) Lightning rarely strikes the same place twice.

   c) My mom made coffee and sandwiches for her book club friends.

   d) The clouds floating by quickly turned dark and stormy.

3. Circle the **simple subject** and underline the **simple predicate**.

   a) The tall giraffe pulled the leaves off the top of the tree with its long tongue.

   b) Silver minnows in the stream glittered in the sunshine.

   c) The long dark seaweed swayed gently in the ocean current.

   d) The patch of sunshine on the carpet warmed the cat's fur and made it sleepy.

4. Circle the **compound subject** and underline the **compound predicate**.

   a) My father and brother cheered at the baseball game today.

   b) I helped my mother set the table and clear the table at dinnertime.

   c) For lunch today, we ate potato salad and drank lemonade.

   d) Jamie, Chris, and I made notes and worked on our science project together.

Grammar Review Test (continued)

5. Underline the **common nouns** and start the **proper nouns** with **capitals**.

    a) Mr. fitz goes to the bowling alley every tuesday night.

    b) Sasha, amy, and i went to the mall on the weekend.

    c) Someday soon, we will all go to the toronto zoo together.

    d) Our class took a field trip to the ontario science centre.

6. Rewrite each sentence, replacing the underlined words with **possessive pronouns**.

    a) Jack's dog is much larger than our dog.

    b) I thought that bike was your bike, but it was actually Kate's bike.

    c) We played ball in our yard because the dog was sleeping in their yard.

    d) This piece of pizza is for me and that piece is for you.

7. Write the **singular** or **plural reflexive** or **intensive pronouns** (e.g., itself, ourselves).

    a) Mitch drew that amazing picture _____.

    b) The cat sat in the sunshine grooming _____.

    c) Battery-powered vacuums move around the house by _____.

    d) Tia told _____ there was nothing to be afraid of.

8. Write the **indefinite pronoun** (e.g., anyone, someone, nobody, everyone).

    a) The lonely stray dog just wanted to find _____ to love him.

    b) _____ could have imagined how severe the flooding would be.

    c) Has _____ seen my glasses? I can't remember where I left them.

    d) _____ was excited about seeing the new movie.

9. Underline the **pronouns** and circle the **antecedents** the pronouns refer to.

   a) Kathy was late again, so we stood outside waiting for her.

   b) The muffins had cooled, so she could now pack them away.

   c) Giggles the Clown was happy when people laughed at him.

   d) Mittens swatted the ball and it rolled under the couch.

10. Does the sentence have an **unclear antecedent**? Circle **Yes** or **No**.

   a) Lisa read the same book as Jody but she didn't finish it. **Yes No**

   b) Karl got high marks on his grammar test. **Yes No**

   c) Tim talked with Dad about his hiking adventure. **Yes No**

   d) I took the cereal out of the box and put it on the table. **Yes No**

11. Circle the **pronoun** that makes the pronoun and its antecedent **agree in number**.

   a) Raccoons came into our yard and (she they) ate our dog's food.

   b) When they told us to bring coats, Bill and I didn't listen to (you them).

   c) When the teacher speaks to the class, we pay attention to (him them).

   d) Dad decorated my birthday cake the way (me I) like it: with sprinkles!

12. Make the sentence **plural** to avoid using **pairs of pronouns**.

   a) When someone speaks to a group, he or she should take a deep breath to calm down first.

   _____

   b) A person should not touch a strange dog because he or she might bite.

   _____

c) A person cannot eat foods that he or she is allergic to.

_____

d) The traveller should make sure he or she charges the cell phone before the trip.

_____

13. Circle **ADJ** if the bold word is an adjective, or **N** if the bold word is a noun.

a) We can ride the **horses** tomorrow if it doesn't rain. **ADJ N**

b) Ted dropped his shiny new dime down the **storm** drain. **ADJ N**

c) Many people feel there is too much **violence** in professional sports. **ADJ N**

d) **Neighbourhood** barbecues are a fun way to meet new neighbours. **ADJ N**

14. Decide whether the underlined word is used as an **adjective or adverb**. Then complete the next sentence.

a) Birds scatter <u>quickly</u> when a hawk appears.

   Quickly is an _____ describing the _____.

b) Male pufferfish make <u>complex</u> patterns with their bodies on the ocean floor.

   Complex is an _____ describing the _____.

c) Sara and Jen arrived an hour <u>early</u> for the concert.

   Early is an _____ describing the _____.

d) The <u>wealthy</u> businessman gave a lot of his money to charity.

   Wealthy is an _____ describing the _____.

15. Circle the **action verbs**. Underline the **linking verbs** and any **helping verbs**.

a) Our class project might be in the front hall science display this year.

b) I was walking to the store, when a sudden gust of wind blew my list away.

c) Most of the boys are taller than the girls in my class.

d) Little white clovers grow in my backyard and they look pretty.

16. Underline the **action verb** and circle the **direct object or objects**.

a) The dog chased the grey squirrel up a tree.

b) Sanjay counted 100 nickels from his piggy bank.

c) My dad and I baked brownies and cookies this weekend.

d) The boys and girls all learned to knit yesterday.

17. Underline the **direct object** and circle the **indirect object**.

a) The man brought his books back to the library.

b) Red squirrels collect pinecones for winter food.

c) The gorilla used leaves to make a nest.

d) My family cleaned up the garden for my grandmother.

18. Add **quotation marks** to each sentence. Add **commas** where necessary.

a) May I try this dress on? the girl asked the saleslady.

b) Jim said We need to stop to eat lunch now.

c) We're going to the post office first said Mom then we'll go to the mall.

d) That's our ball! the boys shouted at the dog.

19. Add **commas** where necessary.

a) Lions tigers and leopards are three types of big cats.

b) Jim is my youngest cousin isn't he?

c) "You gave a great performance as a shark in the play Jeff" Grandpa said.

d) In Toronto Ontario the Hockey Hall of Fame is a popular tourist attraction.

20. Add a **colon** or a **semicolon** where necessary.

    a) I have two favourite movies Finding Nemo and Over the Hedge.

    b) It was very icy outside I slipped and fell on my knees.

    c) Tuesday is my birthday we're all going rock climbing.

    d) Bob is afraid of spiders, heights, and lions.

21. Circle the **correct word** for each sentence.

    a) I felt (bad badly) that Kira's cat didn't like me.

    b) We found a (real really) old coin in Dad's collection.

    c) I answered the questions (bad badly) on the quiz.

    d) Sandy didn't feel (good well) so she stayed home from school today.

22. Underline the **double negatives**. Rewrite the sentence with only one negative.

    a) I never ate nothing for lunch today.

    _____

    b) You don't never share your toys with me.

    _____

    c) I can't go nowhere without this cat following me.

    _____

    d) You won't tell nobody my secret, will you?

    _____

Achievement Award – Canadian Grammar Practice Grade 6

FANTASTIC WORK!

NAME

Achievement Award – Canadian Grammar Practice Grade 6

GREAT GRAMMAR!

NAME

Answers

Types of Sentences, pp. 2–4

(a) imperative; add period (b) interrogative; add question mark (c) exclamatory; add exclamation mark OR declarative; add period (d) declarative; add period (e) imperative; add period (f) interrogative; add question mark (g) exclamatory; add exclamation mark (h) declarative; add period (i) interrogative; add question mark (j) imperative; add period (k) exclamatory; add exclamation mark OR declarative; add period (l) interrogative; add question mark (m) imperative; add period OR declarative; add period OR exclamatory; add exclamation mark (n) imperative; add period (o) interrogative; add question mark

Complete Subjects and Complete Predicates, pp. 5–8

1. Underline the following words: (a) Colourful fireworks (b) The hungry lion (c) The passengers on the train (d) The loud barking of the dog next door (e) My mischievous cousins from Detroit (f) That part of the movie was so scary (g) The roaring race car (h) Hundreds of excited people (i) Her beautiful wavy hair
2. Underline the following words: (a) flew the plane right across the Atlantic Ocean (b) slithered into the shade under a rock (c) made me feel happy (d) reflected off the windows of the houses (e) folds out into a bed (f) ski in the mountains (g) tumbled and twirled in the wind (h) moved quickly around the field in one large group (i) closes down at the end of this week
3. Draw a vertical line between the following words: (a) children wear (b) Patricia sings (c) dots keeps (d) team sprained (e) book describe (f) game made
4. Circle the following: (a) complete subject (b) complete predicate (c) complete predicate (d) complete subject (e) complete subject (f) complete predicate (g) complete predicate (h) complete subject (i) complete predicate

More About Complete Subjects and Complete Predicates, pp. 9–10

1. Underline the following words: (a) Mr. Gibbons, the owner of the house across the street (b) The number of wild giraffes in the world (c) This charm bracelet, a gift from my parents (d) Thousands of communication satellites in space (e) This historic building, once a post office (f) People who never trust others (g) Some baby spiders (h) This piece of amethyst, from a mine in Thunder Bay (i) The idea of the world's tallest mountain
2. Underline the following words: (a) recently discovered the bones of a huge prehistoric snake (b) may become the site of a new shopping mall (c) has been spotted near the outer edge of our solar system (d) cautiously walked along the icy sidewalk (e) gradually rose above the snow-covered mountaintops (f) came up on the girl's forehead where the ball hit her (g) is see a movie with my whole family (h) being kind to others is a way to be kind to yourself
3. Draw a vertical line between the following words: (a) experiments were (b) researchers may (c) aunt sometimes (d) lawn has (e) kindergarten will (f) poodle gave (g) people research (h) America enjoy
4. Circle the following: (a) complete subject (b) complete predicate (c) complete subject (d) complete predicate (e) complete subject (f) complete predicate (g) complete predicate (h) complete subject

Simple Subjects and Simple Predicates, pp. 11–13

1. Circle the following words: (a) book (b) joke (c) avalanche (d) swimmer (e) hippopotamus (f) starlings (g) children (h) scarves
2. Circle the following words: (a) houses (b) photo (c) conductor (d) I (e) toe (f) pencils (g) girl (h) book (i) newspapers
3. Circle the following words: (a) gather (b) questioned (c) should have worked (d) are excavating (e) often take (f) were eating (g) always cooks (h) just pulled
4. Circle the following words: (a) crawled (b) will be landing (c) has been studying (d) completed (e) still ride (f) can see (g) flooded (h) frequently lit up

Compound Subjects and Compound Predicates, pp. 14–15

1. (a) Circle "family" and "friends" and underline "remember"; circle "CS." **(b)** Circle "Water" and underline "dripped" and "landed"; circle "CP." **(c)** Circle "ball" and underline "rolled"; no compound subject or compound predicate. **(d)** Circle "parents," "sister," and "dog"; underline "swam"; circle "CS." **(e)** Circle "He" and "I" and underline "watch"; circle "CS." **(f)** Circle "Sheila" and underline "knocked" and "rang"; circle "CP." **(g)** Circle "shelves" and underline "filled"; no compound subject or compound predicate. **(h)** Circle "Spaghetti" and "lasagna" and underline "were"; circle "CS." **(i)** Circle "Kevin" and "mom"; underline "coughed" and "sneezed"; circle "CS" and "CP." **(j)** Circle "janitor" and underline "mopped" and "emptied"; circle "CP." **(k)** Circle "Mosquitoes" and underline "bit"; no compound subject or compound predicate. **(l)** Circle "earthquake" and underline "destroyed" and "damaged"; circle "CP."
2. (a) Compound sentence **(b)** Compound predicate **(c)** Compound predicate **(d)** Compound sentence

Sentences Review Quiz, pp. 16–17

1. (a) imperative; add period **(b)** interrogative; add question mark **(c)** exclamatory; add exclamation mark **(d)** interrogative; add question mark **(e)** declarative; add period **(f)** imperative; add period
2. Draw a vertical line between the following words: **(a)** cap cheered **(b)** beach is **(c)** me laughed **(d)** candle dripped **(e)** detectives have **(f)** Montreal usually
3. (a) Circle "lions" and underline "chased." **(b)** Circle "Lightning" and underline "flashed." **(c)** Circle "robin" and underline "snatched." **(d)** Circle "ending" and underline "surprised." **(e)** Circle "butterfly" and underline "landed." **(f)** Circle "judges" and underline "announced." **(g)** Circle "portrait" and underline "was donated." **(h)** Circle "perfume" and underline "smells."
4. (a) Circle "ballerinas" and underline "danced" and "leaped"; circle "CP." **(b)** Circle "He" and "she" and underline "are"; circle "CS." **(c)** Circle "Igor" and "parents" and underline "visited"; circle "CS." **(d)** Circle "dandelions" and underline "sprouted" and "spread"; circle "CP." **(e)** Circle "friends" and underline "enjoy"; no compound subject or compound predicate. **(f)** Circle "teacher" and "students"; underline "watched" and "discussed"; circle "CS" and "CP."
5. (a) no check mark **(b)** check mark **(c)** no check mark **(d)** check mark

Common Nouns and Proper Nouns, pp. 18–20

1. (a) Is Aunt Wilma going to paint her <u>house</u>? **(b)** My <u>friend</u> forgot that February is always the shortest <u>month</u>. **(c)** My <u>cousins</u> are all helpful, but Gerald and Nancy are the most helpful. **(d)** A <u>nurse</u> said that Dr. Lopez is moving to Saskatchewan. **(e)** The <u>scientist</u> told the <u>audience</u> that Jupiter is the largest <u>planet</u>. **(f)** My two favourite <u>days</u> of the week are Saturday and Sunday.
2. (a) The Peace Bridge between Canada and the United States was completed in 1927. **(b)** The scientist Marie Curie won the Nobel Prize twice. **(c)** Tourists visit Niagara Falls to see water rushing over steep cliffs. **(d)** Some children speak French at home and English at school. **(e)** A famous racehorse named Northern Dancer won many races. **(f)** My cousin visited the CN Tower on Valentine's Day. **(g)** The planet Mars has two moons, which are named Deimos and Phobos. **(h)** Many castles were built in Europe during the Middle Ages.
3. **(a)** Be sure to ask Dad if we can go the Royal Ontario Museum. **(b)** Did you get your mom a Mother's Day card? **(c)** "My dad taught me to speak Spanish," Mom said. **(d)** "Were you and Mom both born in Westview Hospital?" my sister asked my dad.
4. (a) Police Chief Amanda Knight reported on the criminal's actions. **(b)** Underline "emperor." **(c)** Underline "the queen." **(d)** Mayor Carlos Sanchez held a town hall meeting today.

Possessive Pronouns, p. 21

(a) Nina ate her muffin, but I saved <u>mine</u> for later. **(b)** If this bike were <u>his</u>, he would put new tires on it. **(c)** Mr. Hum's house is larger than <u>ours</u>. **(d)** Our shoes got wet, but <u>theirs</u> stayed dry. **(e)** I lost my ruler, so can I borrow <u>yours</u>? **(f)** I have your address, but I don't have <u>hers</u>. **(g)** Ellen found her key, but <u>mine</u> is still lost. **(h)** I see my parents, but I don't see <u>theirs</u>.

Reflexive and Intensive Pronouns, pp. 22–23

1. **(a)** ourselves **(b)** myself **(c)** themselves **(d)** yourselves **(e)** himself **(f)** itself **(g)** herself **(h)** yourself
2. **(a)** intensive **(b)** reflexive **(c)** reflexive **(d)** intensive **(e)** reflexive **(f)** intensive **(g)** intensive **(h)** reflexive **(i)** intensive

Indefinite Pronouns, pp. 24–26

1. **(a)** no one OR nobody **(b)** everyone OR everybody **(c)** something OR anything **(d)** anyone OR anybody **(e)** everything; nothing **(f)** somebody OR someone **(g)** none **(h)** everything
2. **(a)** customers **(b)** stamps **(c)** cabbages **(d)** eggs **(e)** cookie **(f)** dress
3. **(a)** Underline "each." **(b)** Underline "Many" and circle "few." **(c)** Underline "Both" and circle "one." **(d)** Underline "several" and circle "most." **(e)** Circle "neither." **(f)** Underline "Some" and circle "all." **(g)** Circle "either." **(h)** Underline "All" and circle "some." **(i)** Underline "Enough."
4. **(a)** Circle "few." **(b)** Underline "Most" and circle "several." **(c)** Circle "any." **(d)** Circle "some." **e)** Underline "several" and circle "any." **(f)** Underline "enough." **(g)** Circle "one." **(h)** Underline "Many" and circle "all." **(i)** Underline "Several" and circle "some."

Singular and Plural Indefinite Pronouns, pp. 27–28

1. **(a)** Circle "singular," "singular," and "correct." **(b)** Circle "singular," "plural," and "incorrect." In the example sentence, cross out "work" and write "works." **(c)** Circle "plural," "singular," and "incorrect." In the example sentence, cross out "is" and write "are."
2. Circle the following words: **(a)** looks **(b)** disagree **(c)** knows **(d)** is **(e)** look **(f)** is **(g)** were **(h)** weighs **(i)** is **(j)** succeed **(k)** is

Pronouns and Antecedents, pp. 29–31

1. **(a)** Circle "the puck" and draw an arrow from "it" to "the puck." **(b)** Circle "Gemma" and draw an arrow from "she" to "Gemma." **(c)** Circle "the clothes" and draw an arrow from "them" to "the clothes." **(d)** Circle "Diego and draw an arrow from "him" to "Diego." **(e)** Circle "the book" and draw an arrow from "it" to "the book." **(f)** Circle "Two bears" and draw an arrow from "they" to "Two bears." **(g)** Circle "Tia" and draw an arrow from "she" to "Tia"; circle "a quarter" and draw an arrow from "it" to "a quarter." **(h)** Circle "a sweater" and draw an arrow from "it" to "sweater"; circle "John" and draw an arrow from "him" to "John." **(i)** Circle "Frank, Tony, and Leah" and draw an arrow from "they" to "Frank, Tony, and Leah." **(j)** Circle "a book and a video" and draw an arrow from "them" to "a book and a video." **(k)** Circle "Grapes, apples, and oranges" and draw an arrow from "them" to "Grapes, apples, and oranges." **(l)** Circle "The finches and sparrows" and draw an arrow from "they" to "The finches and sparrows." **(m)** Circle "my brother and my sister" and draw an arrow from "you" to "my brother and my sister."
2. **(a)** Circle "Raj and I" and draw an arrow from "we" to "Raj and I." **(b)** Circle "He and the twins" and draw an arrow from "they" to "He and the twins." **(c)** Circle "Tara, Joan, and I" and draw an arrow from "us" to "Tara, Joan, and I." **(d)** Circle "She and I" and draw an arrow from "we" to "She and I." **(e)** Circle "Dominic" and draw an arrow from "he" to "Dominic"; circle "a hat and a scarf" and draw an arrow from "them" to "a hat and a scarf." **(f)** Circle "Frogs and turtles" and draw an arrow from "they" to "Frogs and turtles." **(g)** Circle "He and she" and draw an arrow from "they" to "He and she." **(h)** Circle "Mia" and draw an arrow from "she" to "Mia"; circle "loonie" and draw an arrow from "it" to "loonie." **(i)** Circle "The puppies" and draw an arrow from "them" to "The puppies." **(j)** Circle "The police" and draw an arrow from "they" to "The police"; circle "the criminals" and draw an arrow from "them" to "the criminals." **(k)** Circle "Grandma" and draw an arrow from "her" to "Grandma"; circle "Timmy and I" and draw an arrow from "we" to "Timmy and I." (l) Circle "Sunshine" and draw an arrow from "it" to "Sunshine."
3. **(a)** Circle "medicine" and draw an arrow from "it" to "medicine." **(b)** Circle "snow" and draw an arrow from "it" to "snow." **(c)** Circle "My cousins" and draw an arrow from "them" to "My cousins." **(d)** Circle "Her grandparents" and draw an arrow from "They" to "Her grandparents"; circle "cat" and draw an arrow from "it" to "cat." **(e)** Circle "Michelle" and draw an arrow from "She" to "Michelle"; circle "Lucy and me" and draw an arrow from "us" to "Lucy and me"; circle "two videos" and draw an arrow from "them" to "two videos." **(f)** Circle "you" and "me" and draw arrows from "We" to "you" and "me."

Canadian Grammar Practice 6 © Chalkboard Publishing

4. **(a)** Circle "Frank," underline "He," and draw an arrow from "He" to "Frank"; Circle "Annie," underline "her," and draw an arrow from "her" to "Annie." **(b)** Circle "The monkeys," underline "They," and draw an arrow from "They" to "The monkeys"; Circle "me and Kerry," underline "us," and draw an arrow from "us" to "me and Kerry." **(c)** Circle "The teacher," underline "She," and draw an arrow from "She" to "The teacher"; circle "I," underline "me," and draw an arrow from "me" to "I." **(d)** Circle "package," underline "it," and draw an arrow from "it" to "package"; circle "my sister and me," underline "We," and draw an arrow from "We" to "my sister and me." **(e)** Circle "Jack, Rita, and I," underline "We," and draw an arrow from "We" to "Jack, Rita, and I"; circle "Lee," underline "him," and draw an arrow from "him" to "Lee." **(f)** Circle "caterpillars," underline "They," and draw an arrow from "They" to "caterpillars"; circle "tree," underline "it," and draw an arrow from "it" to "tree." **(g)** Circle "My cousins" and "my family," underline "we," and draw an arrow from "we" to "My cousins" and to "my family." **(h)** Circle "Lily and Mickey," underline "They," and draw an arrow from "They" to "Lily and Mickey"; circle "the lake," underline "it," and draw an arrow from "it" to "the lake." **(i)** Circle "Tony," underline "He," and draw an arrow from "He" to "Tony"; circle "bag," underline "it," and draw an arrow from "it" to "bag"; circle "marbles," underline "them," and draw an arrow from "them" to "marbles."

Identifying Unclear Antecedents, p. 32

(a) No **(b)** Circle "Yes"; circle "she" and underline "the woman" and "Kate." **(c)** Circle "Yes"; circle "it" and underline "the card" and "the envelope." **(d)** Circle "Yes"; circle "his" and underline "Jim" and "Dad." **(e)** No **(f)** Circle "Yes"; circle "she" and underline "Lisa" and "Victoria." **(g)** No **(h)** Circle "Yes"; circle "he" and underline "Leo" and "uncle."

Correcting Unclear Antecedents, pp. 33–35

1. **(a)** The last scene in the movie was great, so I watched the scene (or "that scene") again and again. **(b)** Theo didn't stay long at Ralph's house because Ralph's aunt was coming to visit.
2. **(a)** While Rani was away, she missed Sue. **(b)** Ahmed watched his goldfish carefully because he knew the cat wanted to eat it. **(c)** The truck had a flat tire after it hit the bus. **(d)** Mom cried tears of joy when she finally saw her sister again. **(e)** Wendy was bored, so Renata played a video game with her. **(f)** Marc shared a pizza with Pierre, who ate three slices.
3. **Note:** *Speaker tags may also appear at the end of a sentence.* **(a)** Mr. Fong told Mr. Prince, "You need a vacation." **(b)** The students told their teachers, "We always work hard." **(c)** Mary told Whiskers, "You are always neat and clean." **(d)** Tim told Mitch, "I'm going to eat hotdogs for lunch." **(e)** The girl told her mother, "I need to buy the pretty green dress." **(f)** Dad told Rajesh, "You can hike to the top of the hill easily."

Avoiding Pairs of Pronouns, pp. 36–37

1. **(a)** When students have the flu, they should stay home from school. **(b)** Passengers should take care not to leave their luggage on the train. **(c)** If you see people who look lost, ask them if they need directions. **(d)** When guests are leaving, we thank them for staying at our hotel.
2. **(a)** The car has room for one more person, so I will find out (or "see" or "ask") if a friend wants to come with us. **(b)** We'll hire one new employee, and the manager will provide training. OR: We'll hire one new employee, who will be trained by the manager.

Nouns and Pronouns Review Quiz, pp. 38–39

1. Use capital letters for the following words: **(a)** Montreal, July, French **(b)** Brooklyn Bridge, New York City, Halley's Comet **(c)** Battle of Hastings, England, Middle Ages
2. **(a)** mine **(b)** his **(c)** ours **(d)** yours
3. **(a)** myself **(b)** ourselves **(c)** itself **(d)** yourselves
4. **(a)** reflexive **(b)** intensive **(c)** intensive **(d)** reflexive **(e)** intensive
5. **(a)** Underline "Everybody" and "no one"; circle "likes." **(b)** Underline "anything" and "someone"; circle "is." **(c)** Underline "both" and "several"; circle "have." **(d)** Underline "few"; circle "are."
6. Circle the following words: **(a)** the books **(b)** a deer **(c)** bananas **(d)** Lucy, Jerry, and I
7. **(a)** Yes **(b)** No **(c)** No **(d)** Yes
8. Two possible correct responses: Jane couldn't play catch with Denise because Jane was busy. Jane was busy, so she couldn't play catch with Denise.

Pronoun–Antecedent Agreement: Number, pp. 40–41

1. Circle the following words: **(a)** singular, plural, do not **(b)** plural, plural, do **(c)** singular, plural, do not
2. We thought our daughters might get bored, but they loved the movie. If I made some errors, I will be sure to correct them.
3. Circle the following words: **(a)** they **(b)** it **(c)** she **(d)** them **(e)** they **(f)** them

Compound Antecedents: Number Agreement, p. 42

(a) Underline "Liz or Anna" and circle "her." **(b)** Underline "Gino and Sal" and circle "they." **(c)** Underline "Terry, Cara, and I" and circle "we." **(d)** Underline "Miguel or Tony" and circle "him." **(e)** Underline "my brothers and my dad" and circle "them." **(f)** Underline "a shirt or boots" and circle "them." **(g)** Underline "gloves or mittens" and circle "them." **(h)** Underline "Lena's earrings or bracelet" and circle "it." **(i)** Underline "The kittens and their mother" and circle "they." **(j)** Underline "The teacher or the students" and circle "them."

Pronoun–Antecedent Agreement: Gender, pp. 43–44

(a) Underline "The plant" and write "it"; circle "neuter" and "singular." **(b)** Underline "a police officer" and write "him or her" or "her or him"; circle "neuter" and "singular." **(c)** Underline "The children" and write "they"; circle "neuter" and "plural." **(d)** Underline "your daughter" and write "she"; circle "feminine" and "singular." **(e)** Underline ""Grandpa's" and write "he"; circle "singular." **(f)** Underline "a princess" and write "her"; circle "feminine" and "singular." **(g)** Underline "a new mayor" and write "he or she" or "she or he"; circle "neuter" and "singular." **(h)** Underline "the boys" and write "they"; circle "masculine" and "plural." **(i)** Underline "an older sibling" and write "her or him" or "him or her"; circle "neuter" and "singular."

Number and Gender Agreement Review Quiz, pp. 45–46

1. Circle the following words: **(a)** singular, plural, do not **(b)** plural, plural, do
2. **(a)** Circle "them"; write "comments." **(b)** Circle "they"; write "Mrs. Gupta and her son." **(c)** Circle "them"; write "my cousins." **(d)** Circle "her"; write "the child." **(e)** Circle "it"; write "sheets or pillowcase." **(f)** Circle "they"; write "Franco and Kyle." **(g)** Circle "them"; write "Irene or her parents."
3. **(a)** Underline "The submarine"; write "it." **(b)** Underline "a doctor"; write "he or she" OR "she or he." **(c)** Underline "his daughter"; write "her." **(d)** Underline "My sisters"; write "their." **(e)** Underline "a parent"; write "he or she" OR "she or he."
4. **(a)** When students are not feeling well, they should see the school nurse. **(b)** Voters must cast their votes before 9:00 p.m. on Thursday.
5. **(a)** I need someone to play tennis with on Saturday, so I will find out (or "ask") if a friend wants to play. **(b)** A reporter will interview the new mayor after the election.

Adjective or Noun? pp. 47–48

1. **(a)** noun **(b)** adjective **(c)** adjective **(d)** noun
2. Underline the following words: **(a)** coffee, kitchen **(b)** Air, summer **(c)** *No words underlined.* **(d)** art **(e)** love **(f)** gift, store **(g)** basketball, sports **(h)** chocolate **(i)** bathroom, hotel **(j)** neighbourhood
3. **(a)** noun **(b)** adjective **(c)** adjective **(d)** noun
4. **(a)** Underline "lottery"; circle "poor" and "sick." **(b)** Underline "blood" and "body." **(c)** Circle "English" and "French." **(d)** Underline "bread" and "spaghetti." **(e)** Underline "computer," "desktop," and "family." **(f)** Underline "government"; circle "unemployed." **(g)** Circle "strong." **(h)** Underline "bicycle" and "head." **(i)** Underline "victory."

What Can Adverbs Describe? pp. 49–51

1. **(a)** Circle "now" and underline "leave." **(b)** Circle "here" and underline "stop." **(c)** Circle "sometimes" and underline "considers." **(d)** Circle "always" and underline "jumps." **(e)** Circle "loudly" and underline "giggled." **(f)** Circle "happily" and underline "skipped." **(g)** Circle "quickly" and underline "talked"; circle "barely" and underline "understand." **(h)** Circle "quickly" and "quietly" and underline "walk." **(i)** Circle "sadly" and underline "meowing." (j) Circle "slowly" and underline "sipped."

2. **(a)** Circle "rather" and underline "disappointed." **(b)** Circle "extremely" and underline "cold." **(c)** Circle "very" and underline "difficult." **(d)** Circle "least" and underline "expensive." **(e)** Circle "very" and underline "carefully." **(f)** Circle "most" and underline "colourful." **(g)** Circle "always" and underline "friendly." **(h)** Circle "last" and underline "spelling." **(i)** Circle "light" and underline "golden." **(j)** Circle "fluffy" and underline "soft." **(k)** Circle "incredibly" and underline "strong."
3. **(a)** Circle "nearly" and underline "perfectly." **(b)** Circle "unusually" and underline "slowly." **(c)** Circle "quite" and underline "easily." **(d)** Circle "very" and underline "formally." **(e)** Circle "almost" and underline "always." **(f)** Circle "never" and underline "really." **(g)** Circle "frequently" and underline "heavily." **(h)** Circle "extremely" and underline "quickly." **(i)** Circle "very" and underline "happily."
4. **(a)** adverb **(b)** adjective **(c)** adverb **(d)** verb **(e)** adjective

Adjective or Adverb? pp. 52–53

(a) adverb; adjective "convincing" **(b)** adverb; verb "hunched" **(c)** adjective; noun "train" **(d)** adverb; verb "aim" **(e)** adjective; noun "solution" **(f)** adjective; noun "temperatures" **(g)** adverb; verb "walk" **(h)** adverb; verb "arrive" **(i)** adjective; noun "work" **(j)** adverb; verb "flew" **(k)** adjective; noun "bus" **(l)** adverb; verb "hit" **(m)** adjective; noun "bath" **(n)** adverb; adjective "intelligent"

Adjectives and Adverbs Review Quiz, pp. 54–56

1. **(a)** adjective **(b)** noun **(c)** noun **(d)** adjective **(e)** adjective **(f)** noun **(g)** adjective **(h)** noun
2. Underline the following words: **(a)** computer **(b)** beef; toaster **(c)** sidewalk **(d)** chocolate; apple **(e)** hardware; light **(f)** metal; hall **(g)** tennis; stone **(h)** plastic; sand **(i)** organ; church
3. **(a)** noun **(b)** adjective **(c)** adjective **(d)** noun **(e)** adjective **(f)** noun **(g)** noun **(h)** adjective
4. **(a)** Underline "bathtub." **(b)** Circle "young" and "elderly." **(c)** Underline "patio" and "winter." **(d)** Circle "wealthy" and underline "sports." **(e)** Circle "hopeful." **(f)** Underline "gel" and "note." **(g)** Circle "tough." **(h)** Circle "strawberry." **(i)** Underline "night" and "alarm."
5. **(a)** adverb **(b)** adjective **(c)** adverb **(d)** adjective **(e)** adverb **(f)** adverb **(g)** adjective **(h)** adjective
6. **(a)** adjective **(b)** verb **(c)** adverb **(d)** adverb **(e)** verb **(f)** adjective **(g)** adjective **(h)** verb

Action Verbs and Linking Verbs, pp. 57–58

1. **(a)** Underline "baby" and circle "cute"; circle "an adjective." **(b)** Underline "Mr. Kapoor" and circle "principal"; circle "a noun." **(c)** Underline "recipes" and circle "complicated"; circle "an adjective." **(d)** Underline "people" and circle "rude"; circle "an adjective." **(e)** Underline "Mrs. Robertson" and circle "teacher"; circle "a noun." **(f)** Underline "accident" and circle "reason"; circle "a noun."
2. **(a)** Underline "might be" and circle "hero." **(b)** Underline "should be" and circle "shorter." **(c)** Underline "did seem" and circle "irritated." **(d)** Underline "are being" and circle "quiet." **(e)** Underline "could be" and circle "clue." **(f)** Underline "might seem" and circle "silly." **(g)** Underline "will be" and circle "athlete." **(h)** Underline "would be" and circle "better." **(i)** Underline "have been" and circle "gone."

More Linking Verbs, pp. 59–60

1. **(a)** action verb **(b)** linking verb **(c)** linking verb **(d)** action verb **(e)** action verb **(f)** linking verb **(g)** action verb **(h)** linking verb **(i)** action verb
2. **(a)** Underline "might become"; linking verb **(b)** Underline "has been"; linking verb **(c)** Underline "will sound"; action verb **(d)** Underline "had proven"; action verb **(e)** Underline "must stay"; linking verb **(f)** Underline "should remain"; linking verb **(g)** Underline "might appear"; action verb **(h)** Underline "looked"; action verb **(i)** Underline "looked"; linking verb **(j)** Underline "went"; linking verb

Direct Objects of Verbs, pp. 61–62

1. **(a)** Underline "collected" and circle "the quizzes." **(b)** Underline "discovered" and circle "fossils." **(c)** Underline "ate" and circle "lunch." **(d)** Underline "damaged" and circle "the library and the hospital." **(e)** Underline "set" and circle "fire." **(f)** Underline "won" and circle "the championship game and a trophy." **(g)** Underline "prescribed" and circle "medicine." **(h)** Underline "covered" and circle "the streets, sidewalks, and cars." **(i)** Underline "watched" and circle "*The Wizard of Oz.*"

2. (a) Underline "painted" and circle "the garage." **(b)** Underline "put" and circle "a sandwich, yogurt, and an apple." **(c)** Underline "feel." ("Feel" is a linking verb here, so there is no direct object.) **(d)** Underline "examined" and circle "the fossil." **(e)** Underline "played." **(f)** Underline "rescued" and circle "a man and a child." **(g)** Underline "wrote" and circle "a story." **(h)** Underline "was." ("Was" is a linking verb, so there is no direct object.) **(i)** Underline "seemed." ("Seemed" is a linking verb, so there is no direct object.)

Indirect Objects of Verbs, pp. 63–64

1. (a) Underline "stories" and circle "the children." **(b)** Underline "his coupons" and circle "the cashier." **(c)** Underline "a song" and circle "their parents." **(d)** Underline "a gift" and circle "her husband." **(e)** Underline "a dress" and circle "Connie." **(f)** Underline "photos" and circle "Hans." **(g)** Underline "shoes" and circle "my sister."
2. (a) Underline "costumes" and circle "us." **(b)** Underline "the ball" and circle "me." **(c)** Underline "the letter." **(d)** Underline "flowers." **(e)** Underline "her change" and circle "Yu." **(f)** Underline "milk." **(g)** Underline "tickets" and circle "us." **(h)** Underline "nuts." **(i)** Underline "a note" and circle "his partner." **(j)** Underline "suggestions" and circle "her team." **(k)** Underline "vegetables." **(l)** Underline "breakfast" and circle "their father."

Verbs Review Quiz, pp. 65–67

1. (a) action verb **(b)** linking verb **(c)** linking verb **(d)** action verb **(e)** action verb **(f)** linking verb **(g)** action verb **(h)** linking verb
2. (a) Circle "Karen"; double underline below "leader" **(b)** Circle "consequences"; single underline below "serious" **(c)** Circle "Mr. Walker"; double underline below "engineer" **(d)** Circle "hard work"; single underline below "worthwhile" **(e)** Circle "project"; single underline below "science" **(f)** Circle "Tao"; single underline below "My friend" **(g)** Circle "Spring"; double underline below "season" **(h)** Circle "mother"; single underline below "busy"
3. (a) No underline **(b)** Underline "did taste" **(c)** Underline "felt" **(d)** Underline "appeared" **(e)** Underline "will become" **(f)** No underline **(g)** No underline **(h)** Underline "look" **(i)** Underline "could be" **(j)** Underline "appeared to be" **(k)** No underline **(l)** Underline "must be" **(m)** Underline "smells" **(n)** No underline **(o)** Underline "sounds" **(p)** Underline "will become"
4. (a) Circle "packed" and underline "china" and "glasses." **(b)** Circle "put" and underline "clothes." **(c)** Circle "removes" and underline "stain." **(d)** No action verb or direct object. **(e)** Circle "raced." **(f)** No action verb or direct object. **(g)** Circle "cut" and "watered"; underline "grass" and "garden." **(h)** Circle "Hold" and "dive"; underline "breath." **(i)** Circle "washed" and underline "hands" and "face."
5. (a) Underline "your ideas" and circle "me." **(b)** Underline "collar" and circle "the dog." **(c)** Underline "his hat." **(d)** Underline "a new bookshelf" and circle "us." **(e)** Underline "best wishes" and circle "Mrs. St. Pierre." **(f)** Underline "an invitation" and circle "the mayor." **(g)** No direct or indirect object. (h) Underline "the blue suitcase." **(i)** Underline "tickets" and circle "me." **(j)** Underline "two comic books" and "a novel"; circle "my friend."

Punctuating Dialogue, pp. 68–69

1. (a) "Could you tell me if there is a gas station nearby?" the driver asked. **(b)** The salesperson said, "This shirt is also available in blue and green." **(c)** "Get off of my lawn!" the woman shouted angrily at the children. **(d)** "Please speak louder so everyone can hear," the teacher requested. **(e)** The plumber said, "I have replaced the leaky pipe in the basement." **(f)** "I have so much homework to do tonight," groaned Paul. (An exclamation point could be used instead of a comma after "tonight.") **(g)** "Who was making all that noise?" Mom asked us. **(h)** "The experts said that finding a solution would take time," reported the mayor. **(i)** "We won the game! We won!" the players cheered loudly.
2. (a) "When I was your age," said Grandma, "people used typewriters because nobody had computers at home." **(b)** "If you want to become successful," the speaker explained, "you must work hard and not give up when you become discouraged." **(c)** The coach told the players, "I am so proud of your teamwork in tonight's game." (An exclamation point could be used instead of a period after "game.") **(d)** "Someone once stole this painting," said the museum guide, "but the police caught the thief before he could sell it." **(e)** "You must be kidding!" Sandra exclaimed in amazement when I told her what had happened. **(f)** "How could anyone do such a terrible thing?" the man asked his wife. **(g)** "If you are not sure how to punctuate this sentence," said the teacher, "look back at the examples."

Using Commas, pp. 70–72

1. **(a)** I think Amelia plays soccer, doesn't she? **(b)** Rodrigo had a nap after washing the dishes, drying them, and putting them away. **(c)** Dinosaur Provincial Park in Drumheller, Alberta, is a popular tourist attraction. **(d)** "Lauren, do you need a ride to baseball practice?" I asked. **(e)** We could use glue, nails, or screws to fasten together the two boards. **(f)** No, I can't go to the movies on Thursday evening because I have choir practice. **(g)** "John, you like pasta, don't you?" Mrs. Greenburg asked. **(h)** My grandparents recently moved to Gander, Newfoundland. **(i)** "Yes, I'll call you tomorrow, Uncle Ken," Sam said. **(j)** We visited a seafood festival, the public gardens, and historic sites in Halifax, Nova Scotia. (k) The fossils in the Royal BC Museum in Victoria, British Columbia, are amazing.
2. Correct punctuation is as follows: **(a)** "Lukas asks interesting questions, doesn't he?" the teacher remarked. **(b)** Regina and Saskatoon are two of the largest cities in Saskatchewan. **(c)** "Lindsay, you're going to come with us, aren't you?" Mom asked. **(d)** In Banff, Alberta, the famous Lake Louise and Banff National Park are popular tourist attractions. **(e)** "No, I am not allergic to eggs, peanuts, or lobster," I explained. **(f)** Susie picked up her hat, mittens, and coat but forgot her scarf. **(g)** The apple blossoms were swarming with bees, flies, and other flying insects. **(h)** "Do you want to eat dinner with us, Jeff?" Katy asked.
3. **(a)** "When I was a little girl," said Grandma, "we walked a mile to school every day." **(b)** "I want to go with you!" shouted the girl. **(c)** Tabby's kittens were named Fluffy, Bitsy, Mittens, and Tiger. **(d)** Ken cut up apples, bananas, oranges, and grapes for his fruit salad. **(e)** "I am going to make a fun cake for your birthday," Aunt May said to Mike. **(f)** "Watch out!" the boy warned as he sped past me on his bike. **(g)** "Alice, are you sure you multiplied those numbers correctly?" Dad asked. **(h)** "Nothing could make me unhappy today," said Tony with a smile.

Using Colons and Semicolons, pp. 73–74

1. **(a)** colon **(b)** colon **(c)** semicolon **(d)** colon **(e)** semicolon, semicolon **(f)** No punctuation is needed. **(g)** colon **(h)** semicolon **(i)** No punctuation is needed.
2. **(a)** First sentence uses a semicolon correctly; second sentence uses a semicolon incorrectly. **(b)** First sentence uses a semicolon incorrectly; second sentence uses a semicolon correctly. **(c)** First sentence uses a semicolon correctly; second sentence uses a semicolon incorrectly. **(d)** Both sentences use a semicolon correctly. **(e)** First sentences use a semicolon correctly; second sentence uses a semicolon incorrectly. **(f)** First sentence uses a semicolon incorrectly; second sentence uses a semicolon correctly.

Punctuation Review Quiz, pp. 75–76

1. **(a)** "Science is my favourite subject," said Alison. **(b)** George whispered, "Be quiet so you don't wake the baby." (An exclamation point could be used instead of a period after "baby.") **(c)** "Do you need any help, sir?" Carla asked. **(d)** "I can't believe it's true!" my father exclaimed.
2. **(a)** "Dad needs the car tonight," Mom explained, "so I can't drive you to Mark's house." (The speaker tag "explained Mom" could also be used.) **(b)** "It seems as though I always get blamed," Dawn grumbled, "even when it's not my fault." (The speaker tag "grumbled Dawn" could also be used.) **(c)** "Thank you for entering the talent show," the judge told the contestants, "and I wish you all luck."
3. **(a)** "Gene, you did a great job on this report!" said the teacher. **(b)** My grandmother told me that she was born in Whitehorse, Yukon. **(c)** "Yes, I did enjoy the movie," replied Fernando. **(d)** "We've eaten at this restaurant before, haven't we?" asked Aunt Selma. **(e)** Milk, cheese, and yogurt are all good sources of calcium. **(f)** "Asan, you'll come to the park with us, won't you?" she asked.
4. **(a)** Yes, I can come at 10:15 tomorrow morning. **(b)** We will visit three cities: Ottawa, Ontario; Calgary, Alberta; and Iqaluit, Nunavut. **(c)** The book is called *I Laughed Out Loud: Best Jokes for Kids.*
5. **(a)** First sentence uses a semicolon correctly; second sentence uses a semicolon incorrectly. **(b)** First sentence uses a semicolon incorrectly; second sentence uses a semicolon correctly. **(c)** Both sentences use a semicolon correctly.

What's the Correct Word? pp. 77–79

(a) Circle "good," "adjective," and "pronoun"; write "he." **(b)** Circle "really," "adverb," and "adjective"; write "fun." **(c)** Circle "badly," "adverb," and "verb"; write "built." **(d)** Circle "well," "adjective," and "pronoun"; write "she."

(e) Circle "well," "adverb," and "verb"; write "eat." **(f)** Circle "bad," "adjective," and "noun"; write "children."
(g) Circle "really," "adverb," and "adjective"; write "old." **(h)** Circle "good," "adjective," and "noun"; write "red."
(i) Circle "really," "adverb," and "adjective"; write "beautiful." **(j)** Circle "bad," "adjective," and "noun"; write "milk."
(k) Circle "good," "adjective," and "noun"; write "forecast." **(l)** Circle "bad," "adjective," and "pronoun"; write "I."

Write the Correct Word, pp. 80–81

1. Circle the following words: **(a)** advice **(b)** accept **(c)** effect **(d)** except **(e)** advise **(f)** affect **(g)** accept **(h)** affect **(i)** effect **(j)** advice
2. Circle the following words: **(a)** rise **(b)** Besides **(c)** whether **(d)** raise **(e)** beside **(f)** weather **(g)** rise **(h)** whether **(i)** raise **(j)** besides **(k)** weather

Double Negatives, pp. 82–83

1. **(a)** Underline "Don't" and "nothing"; Don't say anything about the surprise party. OR: Say nothing about the surprise party. **(b)** Underline "couldn't" and "nowhere"; I couldn't find my watch anywhere. **(c)** Underline "won't" and "never"; We will never go to that restaurant again. OR: We won't go to that restaurant again. **(d)** Underline "can't" and "nobody"; You can't trust anyone these days. OR: You can trust no one these days. **(e)** Underline "not" and "no"; That show is not on TV anymore. **(f)** Underline "shouldn't" and "no one"; You shouldn't tell anyone our secret. OR: You should tell no one our secret.
2. **(a)** My sister has freckles, but I don't have any; My sister has freckles, but I have none. **(b)** There is no easy answer to that question; There isn't an easy answer to that question.

Identifying Errors, pp. 84–85

1. **(a)** C **(b)** A **(c)** B, E **(d)** D **(e)** E, G **(f)** G, H **(g)** D **(h)** F, G **(i)** no errors **(j)** B, G **(k)** B, C **(l)** F **(m)** G, H **(n)** A, E **(o)** D
2. On <u>Sunday</u>, Carrie went to her sister Kate's house for lunch. Kate made spaghetti and sauce. Carrie <u>said that she liked spaghetti</u>. Kate brought out everything <u>except</u> the grated cheese. Carrie got the cheese and placed it <u>beside</u> Kate. Halfway through her <u>lunch, Carrie</u> remembered she had an assignment <u>due</u> on <u>Tuesday</u>. Carrie felt <u>bad</u> that she <u>had not done the work</u>. She <u>needed to choose a subject, do some research, and write</u> a report. If <u>she</u> did not hand in the report, it would <u>affect</u> her mark. Carrie's sister <u>advised</u> her to go straight home after lunch and work on her <u>project</u>.
What subject would she <u>choose</u>? Carrie did not know whether she wanted to write about lions or about hippos. She knew a lot about lions, but she <u>didn't know anything</u> about hippos. Carrie chose hippos for a <u>real challenge</u>. She worked hard on her report and handed it in on Tuesday. The next week, Carrie ran to Kate's house to show her the <u>good</u> mark she got on her project. Carrie <u>said she was really happy she had taken Kate's advice</u>.

Correcting Errors: "Disaster Cake," pp. 86–87

Paragraph 1, sentence 1: My sister and I decided to make <u>Dad</u> a birthday cake.
Paragraph 2, sentence 3: "... three <u>ingredients:</u> water, vegetable <u>oil,</u> and eggs," she said.
Paragraph 3, sentence 1: "How do we make the <u>icing?</u>" I asked.
Paragraph 4, sentence 1: "I found a can of <u>icing</u> we can use," she <u>replied.</u>
Paragraph 4, sentence 2: "... <u>except</u> birthday candles."
Paragraph 6, sentence 2: ... into a large <u>bowl,</u> and Lisa added the water and vegetable oil.
Paragraph 6, sentence 4: I hit the first egg <u>too</u> hard against the edge of the bowl.
Paragraph 6, sentence 5: The shell broke into lots of tiny <u>pieces,</u> ....
Paragraph 7, sentence 1: "Don't worry if <u>there are</u> still a few pieces ...," said Rachel.
Paragraph 8, sentence 3: ... but I couldn't <u>hear</u> her because the mixer made a lot of noise.
Paragraph 8, sentence 4: "What did you <u>say?</u>" I asked as I lifted the mixer out of the bowl.
Paragraph 8, sentence 5: I should <u>have</u> turned <u>it</u> off first.
Paragraph 9, sentence 1: "Don't mix it <u>anymore</u>," Rachel said in a frustrated voice.
Paragraph 9, sentence 3: " ... We can clean up the mess you <u>made</u> while the cake bakes."
Paragraph 10, sentence 2: "We forgot to preheat the <u>oven!</u>" she exclaimed.

Paragraph 11, sentence 1: … I <u>smelled (or "smelt")</u> something burning.
Paragraph 12, sentence 3: We don't have <u>any</u> time to let it cool. OR: We <u>have no</u> time … .
Paragraph 12, sentence 4: "… We'll put the icing on <u>right</u> now."
Paragraph 14, sentence 4: We stuck <u>them</u> on the cake anyway.
Paragraph 15, sentence 1: "Happy <u>Birthday,</u> Dad!" we <u>shouted</u> as Mom and Dad <u>came</u> into the <u>kitchen.</u>
Paragraph 15, sentence 3: … as they looked at <u>our</u> creation.
Paragraph 16, sentence 1: "I'm sure it tastes better <u>than</u> it <u>looks.</u>" Dad said.

Vocabulary List 1, pp. 88–89

(a) coaxed (b) boisterous (c) credible (d) obstacle (e) inevitable (f) abundant (g) prefer (h) credible (i) Abundant (j) inevitable (k) boisterous

Vocabulary List 1: Review, p. 90

1. (a) boisterous (b) inevitable (c) abundant (d) credible (e) prefer (f) obstacle
2. (a) coax (b) prefer (c) abundant (d) boisterous (e) inevitable (f) credible (g) obstacle

Vocabulary List 2, pp. 91–92

(a) vowed (b) ample (c) inventory (d) mimic (e) refuge (f) turmoil (g) recuperate (h) vow (i) mimicking (j) ample (k) refuge (l) inventory (m) recuperates

Vocabulary List 2: Review, p. 93

1. (a) vow (b) inventory (c) recuperate (d) mimic (e) turmoil (f) refuge (g) ample
2. (a) mimic (b) vow (c) recuperate (d) inventory (e) ample (f) turmoil (g) mimicked (h) refuge

Vocabulary List 3, pp. 94–95

(a) proficient (b) eavesdropping (c) consented (d) baffled (e) expanse (f) exotic (g) baffling (h) anguish (i) eavesdropping (j) consent (k) anguish (l) proficient (m) exotic

Vocabulary List 3: Review, p. 96

1. (a) proficient (b) expanse (c) anguish (d) exotic (e) consent (f) baffling (g) eavesdrop
2. (a) consented (b) proficient (c) expanse (d) exotic (e) baffling (f) consent (g) eavesdropped (h) anguish

Vocabulary List 4, pp. 97–98

(a) apprehensive (b) feuded (c) hoax (d) quench (e) beneficial (f) duplicate (g) hardy (h) feud (i) duplicate (j) beneficial (k) quench (l) apprehensive

Vocabulary List 4: Review, p. 99

1. (a) hoax (b) duplicate (c) hardy (d) feud (e) apprehensive (f) beneficial (g) quench
2. (a) duplicate (b) feud (c) hoax (d) hardy (e) beneficial (f) duplicate (g) apprehensive

Vocabulary List 5, pp. 100–101

(a) indispensable (b) ignited (c) pedestrian (d) obvious (e) corridor (f) liberate (g) accumulated (h) pedestrian (i) indispensable (j) liberated (k) accumulated (l) corridor

Vocabulary List 5: Review, p. 102

1. (a) obvious (b) ignite (c) indispensable (d) liberate (e) accumulate (f) pedestrian (g) corridor
2. (a) accumulated (b) obvious (c) corridor (d) liberate (e) indispensable (f) pedestrian (g) ignite

Grammar Review Test, pp. 103–108

1. **(a)** Add an exclamation mark; exclamatory **(b)** Add a period; imperative **(c)** Add a question mark; interrogative **(d)** Add a period; declarative

2. **(a)** Circle "The quick brown fox" and underline "jumped over the lazy dog." **(b)** Circle "Lightning" and underline "rarely strikes the same place twice." **(c)** Circle "My mom" and underline "made coffee and sandwiches for her book club friends." **(d)** Circle "The clouds floating by" and underline "quickly turned dark and stormy."

3. **(a)** Circle "giraffe" and underline "leaves." **(b)** Circle "minnows" and underline "glittered." **(c)** Circle "seaweed" and underline "swayed." **(d)** Circle "sunshine" and underline "fur."

4. **(a)** Circle "My father and brother" and underline "cheered." **(b)** Circle "I" and "my mother" and underline "set the table" and "clear the table." **(c)** Underline "ate potato salad" and "drank lemonade." **(d)** Circle "Jamie, Chris, and I" and underline "made notes" and "worked on our science project together."

5. **(a)** Put capitals on "Fitz" and "Tuesday" and underline "bowling alley." **(b)** Put capitals on "Amy" and "I" and underline "mall" and "weekend." **(c)** Put capitals on "Toronto Zoo" and underline "Someday." **(d)** Put capitals on "Ontario Science Centre" and underline "class" and "field trip."

6. **(a)** <u>His</u> dog is much larger than <u>ours</u>. **(b)** I thought that bike was <u>yours</u>, but it was actually <u>hers</u>. **(c)** We played ball in <u>our</u> yard because the dog was sleeping in <u>theirs</u>. **(d)** This piece of pizza is <u>mine</u> and that piece is <u>yours</u>.

7. **(a)** himself **(b)** itself **(c)** themselves **(d)** herself

8. **(a)** someone **(b)** No one **(c)** anyone or someone **(d)** Everyone

9. **(a)** Underline "her" and circle "Kathy." **(b)** Underline "them" and circle "muffins." **(c)** Underline "him" and circle "Giggles the Clown." **(d)** Underline "it" and circle "ball."

10. **(a)** Yes **(b)** No **(c)** Yes **(d)** Yes

11. Circle the following pronouns: **(a)** they **(b)** us **(c)** him **(d)** I

12. **(a)** When people speak to a group, they should take a deep breath to calm down first. **(b)** People should not touch strange dogs because they might bite. **(c)** People cannot eat foods that they are allergic to. **(d)** Travellers should make sure they charge their cell phones before the trip.

13. **(a)** noun **(b)** adjective **(c)** noun **(d)** adjective

14. **(a)** adverb; verb "scatter" **(b)** adjective; noun "patterns" **(c)** adverb; verb "arrived" **(d)** adjective; noun "businessman"

15. **(a)** Underline "might be" **(b)** Circle "walking" and "blew"; underline "was" **(c)** Underline "are" **(d)** Circle "grow"; underline "look"

16. **(a)** Underline "chased"; circle "the grey squirrel" **(b)** Underline "counted"; circle "100 pennies" **(c)** Underline "baked"; circle "brownies and cookies" **(d)** Underline "learned"; circle "to knit"

17. **(a)** Underline "his books"; circle "the library" **(b)** Underline "pinecones"; circle "winter food" **(c)** Underline "leaves"; circle "a nest" **(d)** Underline "the garden"; circle "my grandmother"

18. **(a)** "May I try this dress on?" the girl asked the saleslady. **(b)** Jim said, "We need to stop to eat lunch now." **(c)** "We're going to the post office first," said Mom, "then we'll go to the mall." **(d)** "That's our ball!" the boys shouted at the dog.

19. **(a)** Lions, tigers, and leopards are three types of big cats. **(b)** Jim is my youngest cousin, isn't he? **(c)** "You gave a great performance as a shark in the play, Jeff" Grandpa said. **(d)** In Toronto, Ontario, the Hockey Hall of Fame is a popular tourist attraction.

20. **(a)** I have two favourite movies: *Finding Nemo* and *Over the Hedge*. **(b)** It was very icy outside; I slipped and fell on my knees. **(c)** Tuesday is my birthday; we're all going rock climbing. **(d)** No colon or semicolon needed.

21. Circle the following: **(a)** bad **(b)** really **(c)** badly **(d)** well

22. **(a)** I didn't eat anything for lunch today. **(b)** You never share your toys with me. OR You don't ever share your toys with me. **(c)** I can't go anywhere without this cat following me. **(d)** You won't tell anyone my secret, will you?

  Canadian Grammar Practice 6 © Chalkboard Publishing